Praise for Enduring

"Suffering. You're either in it, ~~you~~ ~~~~~~~~ ~~~~ cal, Scott LaPierre's latest book reveals a gracious pastor's heart, compassionately equipping people for trials. Every believer needs this book."

Douglas Bond—Speaker, tour leader, and author of twenty-five books of biography, practical theology, and historical fiction

"Everywhere we look there are extreme circumstances: hurricanes, fires, earthquakes, diseases, economic challenges, political turmoil, and the list goes on. I truly believe Scott has written a book 'for such a time as this.' This is one of the best biblical treatments on the difficult subject of suffering that I have come across. Packed with encouragement from the Holy Scriptures, Pastor Scott carefully lifts up the wonderful sovereignty of God in suffering and the cross of Christ during trials to help the reader develop the blessing of an eternal perspective. Every believer needs this volume in their library. I wholeheartedly recommend *Enduring Trials God's Way!*"

Carlton C. McLeod, D. Min—Speaker, author, and senior pastor of Calvary Revival Church Chesapeake

ENDURING TRIALS GOD'S WAY

ENDURING TRIALS GOD'S WAY

A Biblical Recipe for
Finding Joy in Suffering

Scott LaPierre

www.scottlapierre.org | scott@scottlapierre.org

ISBN: 0999555103
ISBN 13: 978-0999555101
Library of Congress Control Number: 2017917559
Charis Publishing

Unless otherwise indicated all Scripture quotations are taken from the New King James Version®. Copyright © 1982 by Thomas Nelson. Used by permission. All rights reserved.

Abbreviations used for other versions:

- ESV—The ESV® Bible copyright © 2001 by Crossway, a publishing ministry of Good News Publishers. ESV® Text Edition: 2011.
- NASB—Scripture taken from the NEW AMERICAN STANDARD BIBLE®, Copyright © 1960, 1962, 1963, 1968, 1971, 1972, 1973, 1975, 1977, 1995 by The Lockman Foundation.
- NIV—THE HOLY BIBLE, NEW INTERNATIONAL VERSION®, NIV® Copyright © 1973, 1978, 1984, 2011 by Biblica, Inc. ®

Scripture quotations with brackets, parentheses, or italics are the emphasis of the author.

Dedication

Enduring Trials God's Way is dedicated to my children.

Dear Rhea, Ricky, Johnny, Charis, Chloe, Noah, and Ruby,

You are seven of God's greatest blessings, and you bring me joy despite any trials I am enduring. As "the children God has graciously given me" (Genesis 33:5b), you are some of the most wonderful manifestations of the Lord's favor in my life.

Your mother and I have prayed for your salvation since the day you were born. Our strongest desire has been, and will always be, for each of you to grow up loving and serving the Lord. When you are "grieved by various trials [may they be opportunities] to prove the genuineness of your faith" (1 Peter 1:6–7).

I love you so much,
Daddy

Acknowledgments

First, I want to thank Stacy Mouat, Kirk VanGelder, Kandie Schmitz, Michelle Templin, and Lori Anderson for serving as beta readers, and Pam Lagomarsino for going above and beyond as my editor. All your thoughts and suggestions were invaluable.

Second, I want to thank the wonderful congregation at Woodland Christian Church. This book came from sermons I preached on trials, and your hunger for God's Word encouraged me in my studying each week.

Third, I want to thank my wonderful wife, Katie. You help me in all ways, including easing the trials I face. "Many women have done excellently, but you surpass them all" (Proverbs 31:29). I love you more now than I did on our wedding day.

Finally, I want to thank my Lord and Savior, Jesus Christ. You are our example in trials, "enduring the cross for the joy that was set before You" (Hebrews 12:2).

Table of Contents

Introduction

My wife, Katie, and I grew up together in northern California. We lost touch after high school and then reconnected almost ten years later. At the time, Katie was living in our hometown of McArthur, California, but I was seven hours south in Lemoore, California. Some wonderful friends of mine, Pat and Kathy Mundy, graciously invited Katie to live with them so we could be near each other, even though they did not know her yet. The four of us became close. They performed our pre-marital counseling and made the trip north for our wedding. Seven years ago, Katie and I moved from Lemoore to Woodland, Washington. Although the distance changed our relationship with Pat and Kathy, we remained friends.

A few years ago, Pat retired from the police department, and he and Kathy looked forward to investing in their grandkids, traveling, and serving in the church. Then everything changed. Kathy got sick, and a hospital visit revealed an aggressive form of cancer. The "golden years" have been filled with doctor appointments and multiple rounds of chemotherapy. Nothing slowed the disease, and in a last attempt, they moved to Seattle for an experimental treatment. A few weeks ago, on their way north, they surprised us and stopped by our house to visit.

I felt privileged to see them at this time in their lives. As soon as we got them sitting in our living room, I wanted to hear everything they felt comfortable sharing about their trial, but the first thing they said was, "How is your dad's Alzheimer's?" Despite what they were experiencing, they "[esteemed] others better than [themselves]" (Philippians 2:3). Throughout the conversation, they gave little indication they were experiencing such a difficult test. As we talked, they discussed their blessings far more than they discussed any amount of suffering. Repeatedly, they shared how good God was being to them.

Reflecting on that conversation, I have asked myself: "Why did they not question (or criticize) God? How could they be so thankful during such a difficult trial? Why did they respond this way when their circumstances would devastate many other people? Could I respond this way if I experienced something similar?" Only time can provide an answer to the last question. The other questions I hope to answer in the following chapters.

Is there any reason you should trust my answers? No, and I am not asking you to do so. This book is not a collection of my thoughts about trials. Rather, I am inviting you to trust the Bible. *Enduring Trials God's Way* came from several sermons I preached, and I labored over each one for twenty to thirty hours per week. God knows what is necessary for people to find joy in suffering, and I hope to present the recipe for that in the following chapters.

As a pastor, I watch firsthand as people suffer through trials. Woodland Christian Church maintains a prayer list, and it seems as soon as we can remove one request, another is added. We have prayed about medical issues, job losses, deaths of family members, and the examples could go on.

My family has not been immune to trials. This past year: my sister-in-law, who lives with her family next door to us, experienced two massive heart attacks; my dad, who lives with my mom up the street from us, went through radiation and chemotherapy (and that is besides his Alzheimer's); and Katie and I experienced our second miscarriage.

Trials are inevitable on this side of heaven as we will see as we begin chapter 1. My prayer has been that I can give you the encouragement from God's Word that He wants you to have when you experience them!

Chapter One

Expect Trials

Beloved, do not think it strange concerning
the fiery trial which is to try you,
as though some strange thing happened to you.
—1 Peter 4:12

Peter tells us "not [to] think [trials] strange." The New Testament was primarily written in Greek, and the word for "strange" is *xenizō*. It means, "Surprised, astonished, or shocked."[1] We should not be surprised, astonished, or shocked by trials; instead, we should expect them. James 1:2 says, "*when* you fall into various trials..." versus "*if* you..." We will face trials, and this is a New Testament theme:

- Acts 14:22a—"Strengthening the souls of the disciples, exhorting them to continue in the faith, [Paul said], 'We must through many tribulations enter the kingdom of God.'"

- Thessalonians 3:3—"No one should be shaken by these afflictions; for you yourselves know that we are appointed to this."

Even though trials are part of the Christian life, we often question how they could happen to us. We might say, "Why would God let this take place?" We act surprised, astonished, or shocked, but based on Scripture we should say, "Since I know trials are part of the Christian life, how would God have me respond? How can I handle this in a way that glorifies Him?"

We should go through this life with the understanding that all Christians experience trials. People expecting the Christian life to be carefree are in for a shock. This is why it is terrible to tell people, "If you become a Christian, Jesus will make your life wonderful!" When they experience trials, there are only three possibilities:

1. They will be upset with you later, feeling as though you lied to them.
2. They will be angry with Jesus for not making their life perfect like you said He would.
3. They will think Christianity is untrue, telling themselves, "If Jesus were real, He would not have let this happen to me."

Instead, we need to be honest about trials, encouraging others and ourselves to embrace what Jesus said to His disciples: "In the world *you will have tribulation*" (John 16:33b).

Trials Are Unpredictable, but Not Accidents

Even though we should expect trials, we do not know when they will take place, which makes them unpredictable. James 1:2 says, "My brethren, count it all joy when you *fall into* various trials." The words "fall into" communicate the unexpected nature of trials. The Greek word for "fall into," or other translations say, "face," "meet," or "encounter," is *peripiptō*.[2] It only occurs three times in Scripture and each time it describes something that is unpredictable. The other two occurrences are:

- Luke 10:30—"Jesus answered and said, 'A certain man went down from Jerusalem to Jericho, and fell among (peripiptō) thieves, who stripped him of his clothing, wounded him, and departed, leaving him half dead.'"
- Acts 27:41a—"Striking (peripiptō) a place where two seas met, they ran the ship aground."

It was unexpected when thieves robbed the man and when the boat crashed. Unpredictable is a great way to describe trials, but do not misunderstand the words "fall into" and think trials are accidents. It is not as though we are walking along, trip, and find ourselves in a trial.

If we see trials this way, then when we experience one we will say, "I am so unlucky. Why do bad things keep happening to me?" Even worse is when people feel as though they could have prevented whatever took place. They are filled with guilt and regret saying, "If I had only _____, then this would not have happened." They beat themselves up, sometimes never forgiving themselves.

Instead of viewing trials as accidents, we need to recognize they are from the Lord. Before trials reach us, they first pass through the throne of God. Some people are troubled by this view, but what is the alternative? God is not sovereign. He is not directing our lives. He is not in control of what happens to us. He is looking down saying, "Why did this happen to _____? I wish there were something I could do. If only _____ would have happened instead." This is a troubling view!

If you could only choose one area of life you want God in control of, wouldn't it be the trials you experience? When you are suffering, one of the best ways to encourage yourself and experience any comfort is in recognizing: "God is in control. I can trust Him. He loves me. I am His child. He wants what is best for me, and He is using this for my benefit."

One of the most quoted verses when people are suffering is Romans 8:28: "We know that all things work together for good to those who love God, to those who are the called according to His purpose." This verse is about God's sovereignty. It encourages us because we are reminded the trial we are experiencing is not an accident.

The Need to Be Prepared

Since we should expect trials, we must prepare for them. Asa, king of Judah, provides a perfect illustration. Unfortunately, sometimes people read the Old Testament and think, "What does this have to do with me? How can I learn from people whose lives are so different from mine?" These are unfortunate questions to ask because the New Testament states the Old Testament provides us with examples:

- Romans 15:4a—"For whatever things were written [in the Old Testament] were written *for our learning*."
- 1 Corinthians 10:11a—"Now all these things happened to [the Israelites] *as examples*, and they were written *for our admonition*."

Church Age believers can learn from Old Testament accounts. Often, they provide a backdrop for New Testament instruction. Asa was one good king in the Old Testament, and he reveals how (and when) to prepare for trials. Early in Asa's reign, God gave him peace. What did he do during this restful time? He built! Part of 2 Chronicles 14:5–7 records:

The kingdom was quiet under [Asa]. And *he built* fortified cities in Judah, for *the land had rest; he had no war* in those years, because *the LORD* had given him rest. Therefore he said to Judah, "*Let us build* these cities and make walls around them, and towers, gates, and bars, while the land is yet before us, because we have sought the LORD our God; we have sought Him, and *He has given us rest on every side.*" So *they built* and prospered.

Like Asa, we should build during peaceful times. While Asa strengthened his nation physically, we should strengthen ourselves spiritually. Pray and read the Word regularly. Serve the body of Christ. We do not serve others so they will serve us. We serve others because we want to serve Christ, but one blessing often produced is brothers and sisters who will "weep with [us when we] weep" and "suffer with [us]" when we suffer (Romans 12:15b, 1 Corinthians 12:26a). I have seen people enter trials and become frustrated that nobody was there for them, but in most of those cases they were not there for others who were "weeping" and "suffering."

Unfortunately, during peaceful times, we are often tempted to do the opposite of build, and that is to relax. Then we are unprepared when trials come.

Let me illustrate the danger of this with a sports analogy. I attended a small high school. Our football team had less than twenty players. While I have no doubt I would not have played much at a more competitive school, at my school I was the running back, punt returner, and kickoff returner. As a result, I was often tackled, and it taught me there are two ways to be hit. The most common and desirable way is when it is expected. You know you will be tackled, so you prepare for the hit. The other tackle type takes place when you are blindsided. Since you did not expect to be hit, you are unprepared, and it can be devastating. The point? Sadly, many people are like football players running down the field, unprepared for the trial about to blindside them.

As a pastor, I have seen people become serious about their relationships with the Lord once they are in a trial. Then they begin praying, reading the Bible, and attending church consistently. God uses trials to bring people to Himself, so this is better than not engaging in these spiritual activities; however, this is far from the ideal approach. What if Asa built his nation after an enemy attacked him? Should a student begin studying the day of a test? Should a couple plan for retirement when they retire? Should parents start discipling their children when they become teenagers? Likewise, people should not begin preparing for trials when they are experiencing one.

Athletes and soldiers spend years preparing for competitions and combat. Should Christians compare themselves with athletes and soldiers? Paul thought so! He said a Christian "must endure hardship as a *good soldier of Jesus Christ*…that he may please Him who *enlisted him as a soldier*" (2 Timothy 2:3–4), and he called Epaphroditus and Archippus "fellow soldiers" (Philippians 2:25, Philemon 1:2). We are commanded to wear armor and carry a sword (Ephesians 6:11–17). Paul compared the Christian life to a race (1 Corinthians 9:24–25, 2 Timothy 4:7, Hebrews 12:1). Like athletes and soldiers must prepare physically, so must Christians prepare spiritually. When believers are spiritually lazy, they should expect to struggle with trials as much as physically lazy athletes and soldiers would struggle during combat and athletic competitions.

Moving back to Asa, he strengthened his nation during times of peace, and this left him prepared when the time came. Second Chronicles 14:8–10 continues:

> And Asa had an army of three hundred thousand from Judah who carried shields and spears, and from Benjamin two hundred and eighty thousand men who carried shields and drew bows; all these were mighty men of valor.
>
> Then Zerah the Ethiopian came out against them with an army of a million men and three hundred chariots, and he came to Mareshah. So Asa went out against him, and they set the troops in battle array in the Valley of Zephathah at Mareshah.

We all face trials, and Asa was no exception. One of the most formidable armies recorded in Scripture came against him. His five hundred eighty thousand soldiers sound impressive until you read that the Ethiopians numbered one million. No, we do not face armies that greatly outnumber us, but we do face trials that make us feel as desperate as Asa felt. He was completely distressed, and to his credit, he responded wonderfully. Second Chronicles 14:11–12 records:

> And Asa cried out to the LORD his God, and said, "LORD, it is nothing for You to help, whether with

many or with those who have no power; help us, O LORD our God, for we rest on You, and in Your name we go against this multitude. O LORD, You are our God; do not let man prevail against You!" So the LORD struck the Ethiopians before Asa and Judah, and the Ethiopians fled.

This is what it looks like to turn to the Lord during a difficult trial. Asa praised God's strength and poured out his heart to Him. Write this prayer down. Circle it, highlight it, or underline it in your Bible. Asa's trial was the Ethiopian army, but our trial might be a job loss, cancer diagnosis, unfaithful spouse, or rebellious child. When the trial comes, follow Asa's example and cry out to God for help.

The Greater Victory God Provides

God honored Asa's dependence on Him by fighting on his behalf and striking down the Ethiopians. At this point, I wish I could write: "If you depend on the Lord, He will strike down whatever trial you face. He will give you a better job. He will heal the cancer. He will bring your unfaithful spouse or rebellious child to repentance." The problem is, this would not be true. God might not do any of those things regardless of your spiritual maturity or faith.

In a discussion of the godliest Christians, the Apostle Paul would have to be considered, if not placed at the top of the list. He suffered from "a thorn" that affected him so much he "pleaded with the Lord three times that it might depart from [him]" (2 Corinthians 12:8). In 2 Corinthians 11:23–29, Paul listed his sufferings for Christ, and they included imprisonments, whippings, near-death experiences, beatings, stoning, shipwrecks, sleeplessness, hunger, thirst, and nakedness. This man was acquainted with trials, so for him to pray three times that God would remove something reveals how terrible it must have been. Despite Paul's godliness, instead of removing the thorn, God told him, "My grace is sufficient for you" (2 Corinthians 12:9a). God gave him the grace he needed to endure the difficult trial.

We do not know what the thorn was—whether it was physical, mental, emotional, or spiritual—which allows us to apply it to any suffering we experience. We pray for God to remove trials like Paul prayed for God to remove the thorn. If God does not remove the trial like He did not remove Paul's thorn, then we must also trust God's grace will be sufficient to endure the trial like it was sufficient for Paul to endure the thorn.

The most extreme consequence of a trial is death. What happens if "the thorn" takes our lives—how does that reveal God's sufficiency? In 1 Corinthians 15:26, Paul calls death our "enemy" and then in 1 Corinthians 15:54–57, he writes:

> So when this corruptible has put on incorruption, and this mortal has put on immortality, then shall be brought to pass the saying that is written: "Death is swallowed up in victory."

"O Death, where is your sting?
O Hades, where is your victory?"
The sting of death is sin, and the strength of sin is
the law. But thanks be to God, who gives us the victory through our Lord Jesus Christ.

Death is capitalized to personify it as an enemy that Jesus defeated. Asa faced the Ethiopians, and Death is an
enemy we face. To illustrate the finality of Christ's victory
over Death, Revelation 20:14 says, "Death [is] cast into the
lake of fire." If a trial takes our lives, then God's grace is
sufficient through Christ's victory over Death. Just as God
fought for Asa and gave him the victory over the enemy he
faced, so too has He fought for us and given us the victory
over the enemy we face.

Hebrews 11 contains a collection of the great men and
women of faith. Toward the end of the chapter two groups
are identified. The first group is in verses 33–35a:

Through faith [they] subdued kingdoms, worked
righteousness, obtained promises, stopped the
mouths of lions, quenched the violence of fire, es-
caped the edge of the sword, out of weakness were
made strong, became valiant in battle, turned to
flight the armies of the aliens. Women received their
dead raised to life again.

What a fantastic account of victories! This might be the most condensed list of triumphs in all of Scripture. Immediately after this though, the second group is listed in verses 35b–38:

> Others were tortured…[they] had trial of mockings and scourgings, yes, and of chains and imprisonment. They were stoned, they were sawn in two, were tempted, were slain with the sword. They wandered about in sheepskins and goatskins, being destitute, afflicted, tormented—of whom the world was not worthy. They wandered in deserts and mountains, in dens and caves of the earth.

What a heavy account of sufferings! This might be the most condensed list of defeats in all of Scripture. Why the difference between the two groups? Did the second group lack faith? Were they lesser Christians than the first group? Not at all. They were wonderful men and women of God. For reasons not revealed, God allowed completely different outcomes for two equally faith-filled groups of people. From earth's perspective, it looks as though God did not give the second group victories over the trials they faced, but from heaven's perspective "the world was not worthy" of them. They were too good for this world, so God removed them from it. In Philippians 1:21, Paul said, "For to me, to live is Christ, and *to die is gain*" and they gained the victory of being ushered into heaven.

The Danger of Daily Trials

James 1:2 says, "*You* fall into *various* trials..." and 1 Peter 1:6 says, "*You* have been grieved by *various* trials..." The words "you" and "various" reveal the personal and unique nature of trials. For Asa, he faced an Ethiopian army that was almost twice the size of his army. For others, their trials were considerably different:

- Joseph was betrayed by his brothers and sold into slavery.
- Job lost most of his loved ones and experienced terrible physical suffering.
- David was hunted by King Saul for years.
- Ezekiel's wife was killed.
- The Apostle John was exiled on the island of Patmos.

Each of these trials was personal and unique to the individuals, and the trials we experience are personal and unique to us. Although that creates a similarity between us and the people in Scripture, the problem is we are often given the most dramatic events from their lives. Most trials we experience daily are of a much smaller magnitude. Only a handful of times do we experience suffering that could be considered life-changing. The rest of our lives are filled with trials that could be fittingly described by Jesus: "And the rain descended, the floods came, and the winds blew and *beat on that house*" (Matthew 7:25a and 27a).

What imagery is created by the words "beat on that house"? These are the trials that take place daily and can even become unrecognizable because of their regularity. These storms beat on us at work, home, school, while raising children, and the list goes on until we—like the house in the parable—feel as though we are going to collapse. Who has not said, "I cannot do this anymore! I do not know if I will make it through one more day." Many people have honorably endured great trials, but then found themselves too weak to endure the strain of sleepless nights with babies, unpleasant co-workers, obnoxious neighbors, marriage struggles, financial issues, and health problems.

In November 2015, Czech pilot, Zbynek Abel, was forced to perform an emergency landing of his Aero L-159 Alco subsonic attack jet when it collided with a bird. The aircraft was armed with powerful weapons that could destroy other planes and attack cities, but it was downed by a bird hundreds of times smaller and had no powerful engine, deadly weapons, or skilled pilot.[3] In the same way, small trials can threaten to take us down, making them as dangerous as the large trials we fear most. We know people who have endured great trials, whether it is a disease, physical handicap, or the loss of a loved one. We are challenged by their endurance, wondering how we would respond if we were in their place. Although, this creates a danger if we, like the attack jet, only "arm" ourselves for the large trials of life.

What is the solution to these daily trials? Jesus provided the answer: "whoever hears these sayings of Mine, *and does them*, I will liken him to a wise man who built his house on the rock: and the rain descended, the floods came, and the winds blew and beat on that house; and it did not fall, *for it was founded on the rock*" (Matthew 7:24–25).

Asa needed to build a strong foundation during times of peace to endure the trial of the Ethiopian army that could have collapsed his nation. Similarly, we need a strong foundation to endure the trials that can lead to the collapse of our lives. That foundation is obedience to Christ. Jesus promised obeying His teaching enables us to survive the storms of life we can all expect.

Questions

1. Why should it be encouraging to remember God is in control while you are in the middle of a trial?

2. Have you been "building your walls" during times of peace? If yes, how? If not, how will you build in the future?

3. Discuss three trials you experienced that are common to all Christians.

   A.

   B.

   C.

4. Discuss three trials you experienced that were unique to you.

    A.

    B.

    C.

5. Describe a victory God gave you from a trial.

6. What daily trials do you experience that you need to be aware of, because of their potential to wear you down?

Chapter Two

Did You Do Something Wrong?

For it is better, if it is the will of God,
to suffer for doing good than for doing evil.
—1 Peter 3:17

Y ou should expect trials, but when they take place, you do not have to wonder if you did something wrong! A woman wrote me about a miscarriage she experienced, asking if God was punishing her. It was heartbreaking. The miscarriage was painful enough without also having to wonder if it was her fault. It is tragic when people blame themselves for their trials.

It is also tragic when people experience trials and "friends" try to get them to blame themselves! Job's friends come to mind. They started off well "[sitting] down with him on the ground seven days and seven nights, and *no one spoke a word to him*, for they saw that his grief was very great" (Job 2:13). This demonstrates what to do when people are suffering. The "Ministry of Presence" requires being a good listener. I received a good piece of advice when I first became a pastor: "If you cannot improve on silence, do not." Solomon said there is "A time to keep silence, and a time to speak" (Ecclesiastes 3:7b), and "He who has knowledge spares his words" (Proverbs 17:27a).

Unfortunately, Job's friends did not follow these verses, and things went downhill after they opened their mouths. Eliphaz was the first to speak, and he summarized their argument in Job 4:7 when he asked, "Who ever perished being innocent? Or where were the upright ever cut off?" In other words, "When have bad things ever happened to good people?" Job's friends wanted to convince him that since he suffered terribly, he must have sinned terribly.

As much as Job's friends initially showed what to do when people suffer, they later also showed what not to do—lecture, preach, say things like, "This is happening because…" or worse, "God would not be doing this if you…" At the end of the book, God showed up and "said to Eliphaz the Temanite, 'My wrath is aroused against you and your two friends, for *you have not spoken of Me what is right*'" (Job 42:7). He was referring to their statements that people only suffer when they have done something wrong.

In Jesus' day, people thought if something bad happened it must have been caused by sin. Two accounts reveal that even the disciples held this false belief, and both times they expressed it Jesus corrected them:

- Pilate murdered some Galileans and a tower collapsed causing eighteen deaths. The disciples thought the people died because of their sinfulness, but Jesus said, "Do you suppose that these Galileans were worse sinners than all other Galileans, because they suffered such things? I tell you, no...Or those eighteen on whom the tower in Siloam fell and killed them, do you think that they were worse sinners than all other men who dwelt in Jerusalem? I tell you, no" (Luke 13:2–5).

- When the disciples saw a blind man they asked Jesus: "'Rabbi, who sinned, this man or his parents, that he was born blind?' Jesus answered, 'Neither this man nor his parents sinned, but that the works of God should be revealed in Him'" (John 9:2–3).

God wants to reveal Himself through trials and use them for our good, but we do not have to wonder if we did something wrong. We learned that a trial does not necessarily indicate wrongdoing, but sometimes we do bring on our own suffering.

Do Not Confuse Trials and Discipline

What happens if we suffer because we did something wrong? That is not a trial. That is discipline. The Apostle Peter identifies two causes of suffering: "For it is better, if it is the will of God, to *suffer for doing good than for doing evil*" (1 Peter 3:17). Suffering is part of God's perfect and wise plan for His people even when they do good, but Peter wants his readers to avoid suffering caused by their sinfulness.

As tragic as it is when people experience a trial and wonder if it is their fault, it is equally tragic when people sin, God disciplines them, and they think it is not their fault. Consider these examples from Scripture:

- After Moses struck the rock instead of speaking to it as God commanded, God said, "Because you did not believe Me, to hallow Me in the eyes of the children of Israel, therefore *you shall not bring this assembly into the land* which I have given them" (Numbers 20:12).
- After David committed adultery with Bathsheba and murdered Uriah, God told him through the prophet Nathan, "*The sword shall never depart from your house*, because you have despised Me, and have taken the wife of Uriah the Hittite to be your wife" (2 Samuel 12:10).
- After Jehoshaphat entered an alliance with evil King Ahaziah to build ships, God told him through the

prophet Eliezer, "'Because you have allied yourself with Ahaziah, *the Lord has destroyed your works.*' Then the ships were wrecked" (2 Chronicles 20:37).

These men suffered because of their sins. It would be incorrect to say they experienced trials. It would be correct to say God disciplined them. The same is true of the negative consequences of foolish decisions. Imagine the following:

- People lose their jobs, because they slacked off for years
- People's finances are tight, because of years of impulsive purchases
- People are diagnosed with diabetes, because of years of gluttonous eating
- People are in miserable marriages, because they ignored their parents' warnings about the spouses they married

These are not trials! These are the consequences of exercising poor judgment. These people were "led astray by their own great folly" (Proverbs 5:23b). Sometimes people sin, are disciplined, and then say, "Why am I suffering?" If friends love them enough to be honest, they will answer, "Because of your disobedience."

Although there are rewards for enduring trials (See chapter 6), it is not the same with discipline. When we "[do] evil" and suffer because of it, God expects us to humbly accept it: "For *what credit is it* if, when you are beaten for your faults, you take it patiently?" (1 Peter 2:20a).

Although this might sound discouraging, even though there is no "credit" for receiving discipline there are many benefits! Hebrews 12:11a says, "For the moment all discipline seems painful rather than pleasant." How true are these words! Yes, discipline hurts, but the author of Hebrews also provides reasons believers can be encouraged when disciplined.

When Disciplined: Be Encouraged You Are a Child of God

Hebrews 12:6–8 records:

> "…For the Lord disciplines the one he loves,
> and chastises every son whom he receives."
> It is for discipline that you have to endure. God is
> treating you as sons. For what son is there whom his
> father does not discipline? If you are left without dis-
> cipline, in which all have participated, then you are
> illegitimate children and not sons. (ESV)

When we sin and God disciplines us, we can be encouraged that He does so because He loves us. We want to be confident in our salvation, and experiencing discipline allows us to say, "God is my Father. I am His child." When I see other people's children misbehaving, I do not discipline them because they are not my children. God acts similarly toward unbelievers. Sometimes people sin and it looks like "they are getting away with it." Either God is giving them time to repent, or they are not His children.

When Disciplined: Be Encouraged You Are in God's Hands

Prior to pastoring, I taught elementary school for almost ten years. When students disobeyed, I regularly found myself wondering what the appropriate punishment would be—detention, suspension, time out, or call parents? Circumstances make things even more complicated. What is the punishment for a student who lies once, versus a student who demonstrates a pattern of deceitfulness? What about a student who mistreated a student for no reason, versus a student who acted out when provoked?

Once, when my class was walking in a line, a notoriously cruel student repeatedly flicked another student's ear. This went on for a while, revealing significant self-control from the student being picked on. Finally, he turned around and kicked the bully as hard as he could. What was an appropriate punishment for the student who kicked the other student? Part of me wanted to congratulate him for standing up to someone who intimidated others.

As a parent, I face the same question when disciplining my children. Ephesians 6:4a says, "Fathers, do not provoke your children to wrath." Sometimes I ask myself, "I addressed this with my children before, if I bring it up again, will I be exasperating them?" While Katie and I pray almost daily for wisdom raising our children, we do not know absolutely that we are doing what is right. Hebrews 12:9–10 describes the situation: "We have had human fathers who...*chastened us as seemed best to them*, but *He for our profit*, that we may be partakers of His holiness." As parents, we do what "seems best to us," but when God disciplines us we can be encouraged He is doing what "profits" us. We never have to wonder if He is acting too severely, choosing the wrong punishment, or failing in some other way.

Consider a situation that took place with David after he sinfully numbered the people. God sent the prophet Gad to rebuke him and give him the choice between three different punishments. Second Samuel 24:12–14 records:

> [Gad told] David, "Thus says the LORD: 'I offer you three things; choose one of them for yourself, that I may do it to you.'" So Gad came to David and told him; and he said to him, "Shall seven years of famine come to you in your land? Or shall you flee three months before your enemies, while they pursue you? Or shall there be three days' plague in your land? Now consider and see what answer I should take back to Him who sent me."
>
> And David said to Gad, "*I am in great distress. Please let us fall into the hand of the LORD, for His mercies are great*; but do not let me fall into the hand of man."

When David was disciplined, he wanted to be in God's hands. When we are "in great distress," we can be encouraged that we are in God's hands. He knows what is best.

When Disciplined: Be Encouraged by the Fruit that Can Be Produced

God disciplines us because He wants us to repent. The first thing that comes to mind when thinking about repentance is stopping a sinful action, but repentance is as much about starting (producing fruit), as it is about stopping. John the Baptist said: "Bear fruits worth of repentance" (Matthew 3:8). Ephesians 4:25–32 provides examples of repenting (stopping, putting off), and producing fruit (starting, putting on):

- Ephesians 4:25a—"Therefore, *putting away lying*, 'Let each one of you speak truth with his neighbor.'"
- Ephesians 4:28–29—"Let him who *stole* steal no longer, but rather let him *labor, working with his* hands what is good, that he may have something to give him who has need. Let *no corrupt word* proceed out of your mouth, but what is *good for necessary edification*, that it may impart grace to the hearers."
- Ephesians 4:31–32—"Let all *bitterness, wrath, anger, clamor, and evil speaking be put away from you*, with all malice. And *be kind to one another, tenderhearted, forgiving one another*, even as God in Christ forgave you."

As a pastor, people have asked me, "I repented of _____. Why do I keep struggling?" I respond by asking, "What did you start doing instead? What did you produce in place of your sin?" For example:

- You stopped going to bars, but then how did you spend that time?
- You stopped yelling at your kids, but what did you start saying to them?
- You stopped coveting, but what did you start giving?

There is an unfortunate human tendency for reform to be temporary. Psychologists, prisons, and juvenile centers can testify to this. One main reason is people attempt to repent without producing the corresponding fruit. When sin is removed, the vacuum that is created must be filled. In Matthew 12:43–45a, Jesus told a parable that warns against repentance that leaves a hole:

> When an unclean spirit goes out of a man, he goes through dry places, seeking rest, and finds none. Then he says, "I will return to my house from which I came." And when he comes, he finds it empty, swept, and put in order. Then he goes and takes with him seven other spirits more wicked than himself, and they enter and dwell there; and the last state of that man is worse than the first.

The unclean spirit pictures sin, and the man removed it from his life, but he did not produce fruit. He stopped without starting. He put off without putting on. As a result, his life (the house) remained "empty." Things looked good at first (swept, and put in order), but the spirit (sin) returned and the man's condition was worse. When true repentance has not taken place, inevitably a person's situation deteriorates as the sin grows. We can be encouraged by God's discipline, because it "*yields the peaceful fruit of righteousness* to those who have been trained by it" (Hebrews 12:11b).

Who Benefits from God's Discipline?

The title of the previous section reads, "Fruit that Can Be Produced" versus "Fruit that Is Produced." There is no guarantee God's discipline will benefit us. The end of Hebrews 12:11 says "those who have been trained by it" and this identifies the people who benefit from the Father's discipline. "He will never learn" is a fitting way to describe some people:

- Proverbs 17:10—"Rebuke is more effective for a wise man, than a hundred blows on a fool."
- Proverbs 26:11—"As a dog returns to his own vomit, so *a fool repeats his folly.*"
- Proverbs 27:22—"Though you grind a fool in a mortar with a pestle along with crushed grain, yet *his foolishness will not depart from him.*"

Fools suffer because of their actions, but it does not produce lasting change. Part of the reason is they do not see their fault, because fools never think they are wrong: "The way of a fool is right in his own eyes" (Proverbs 12:15).

There is a similar danger associated with confusing trials and discipline. When people make this mistake, they are acting like fools who fail to see their folly. Without recognizing they caused their suffering, they will not be trained by God's discipline. Why is this the case? If they do not think they have done anything wrong, they will not understand God is trying to produce repentance. Spiritual growth will be hindered, and the painful situation will often be repeated.

When this pattern takes place, the only solution is to have the humility and wisdom to say, "This is not a random trial. I have sinned. God is disciplining me and I must repent." Instead of saying, "How could God let this happen to me?" the proper response is, "I am thankful God loves me enough to get this sin out of my life and help me produce the corresponding fruit."

Questions

1. What is the difference between discipline and a trial? How can you tell the two apart?

2. Have you experienced a trial and thought it was discipline, or discipline and thought it was a trial? Explain.

3. Provide three examples of discipline you personally experienced, and discuss whether it produced repentance and fruit.

    A.

    B.

    C.

4. How can you be encouraged by receiving God's discipline?

5. Why do you think some people benefit from discipline, while others do not?

6. When experiencing discipline, what actions can you take to ensure you benefit from it?

Chapter Three

Count Trials As Joy?!?!

*My brethren, count it all joy when you fall into
various trials, knowing that the testing of your faith
produces patience. But let patience have its perfect
work, that you may be perfect and complete, lacking
nothing.*
—James 1:2–4

James 1:2 uses "joy" and "trials" in the same sentence.
These words do not go together! Who experiences joy
during trials? James even uses the word "all." He does not
say, "Count it *some* joy..." or "Find a *little* joy." He says,
"count it *all* joy." As contrary as this sounds, it is a theme
in Scripture to find joy in trials. Romans 5:3 says, "We glory
in tribulations" and 1 Peter 1:6 says, "In this you greatly
rejoice... [when] you have been grieved by trials." You

might be thinking: "The Bible does not make sense, because I definitely do not feel joy when I am going through a trial!"

The Bible makes complete sense, because it does not say to "feel" joy during trials. Instead, it says "count it all joy," because we cannot go by the way we feel. Trials make us feel sorrow and pain, so we must evaluate them independently of our feelings. The word for "count" is *hēgeomai,* and it means, "To lead, go before, rule, command, have authority over."[4] Here are a few places it is used:

- Matthew 2:6—"Bethlehem...out of you shall come a Ruler (hēgeomai) Who will shepherd My people Israel."
- Acts 7:10—"[Pharaoh] made [Moses] governor (hēgeomai) over Egypt."
- Hebrews 13:17—"Obey those who rule (hēgeomai) over you, and be submissive, for they watch out for your souls, as those who must give account."

James tells us to "count (hēgeomai) it all joy," because we must "govern" and "rule" over trials. We must control the way we view them, versus being controlled by our feelings. We must make a mental judgment about trials by considering the way God wants to use them in our lives. Then we can face them with joy.

The Maturity Trials Produce

We have six children and we recently learned Katie is expecting our seventh. Our oldest child is ten, and while we have enjoyed our children at all ages, we still want to see them mature. When they make decisions that disappoint us, we feel as though they are not maturing quickly enough. Consider how tragic it would be if children remained immature throughout their lives.

God is a Father and He also wants His children to mature. The author of Hebrews rebuked some of his readers who had been following Christ for some time, but had not matured:

> For though *by this time you ought to be teachers*, you need someone to teach you again the basic principles of the oracles of God. *You need milk, not solid food…*Therefore let us *leave the elementary* doctrine of Christ and *go on to maturity*, not laying again a foundation of repentance from dead works and of faith toward God (Hebrews 5:12, 6:1 ESV).

Unlike these Hebrew readers, consider the believers in 2 Thessalonians 1:3–4 who had matured significantly:

> We are bound to thank God always for you, brethren, as it is fitting, because your faith grows exceedingly, and the love of every one of you all abounds toward each other, so that we ourselves boast of you

among the churches of God for your patience and faith *in all your persecutions and tribulations that you endure.*

The Thessalonians were a wonderful church. Paul applauded their growth, which he attributed to the trials they experienced. This is one reason we can find joy in trials—we know they are producing patience that leads to maturity. First Peter 5:10 says, "After you have suffered a little while, [God] will himself restore, confirm, strengthen, and establish you." During trials we can tell ourselves, "This is strengthening me spiritually, giving me endurance, building my faith, and preparing me for the future." Jerry Bridges said, "Every adversity that comes across our path, whether large or small, is intended to help us grow in some way."[5]

The word "patience" suggests waiting, which gives the impression trials make people good at standing in line or waiting at stop lights. Yes, trials can improve our attitudes when we are forced to wait, but that is a poor understanding of the benefit of patience. The Greek word for patience is *hypomonē,* and it means, "The characteristic of a man who is not swerved from his deliberate purpose and his loyalty to faith and piety by even the greatest trials and sufferings."[6]

James 1:4 describes the maturity patience leads to in believers' lives: makes them perfect, complete, and ensures nothing is lacking. Although this sounds like three different benefits of patience, they are synonyms:

- The Greek word for "perfect" is *teleios*, but it does not mean free from mistakes. Instead, it means, "Brought to its end, finished, wanting nothing necessary to completeness."[7]
- The Greek word for "complete" is *holokleros*, which means, "complete in all its parts, in no part wanting or unsound, entire, whole."[8]
- The Greek words for "lacking nothing" are *leipo* (lack, be wanting),[9] *en* (in, by),[10] *medeis* (nobody, nothing).[11]

James 1:4 is not describing three different ways patience helps us; it is describing the maturity patience produces in three different ways.

Patience Allows for Maturity in All Areas of Our Lives

When we suffer, we will sometimes wonder what God is teaching us. We will say things like, "I went through this trial and learned to trust the Lord more," or "This person hurt me and God used the situation to teach me to forgive." We can learn from trials, but that is not the point of James 1:4.

Think of children as they age. They grow overall and not only in select areas. The same is true for believers as they age—or grow—spiritually. There is not one part of our lives that matures. The verse is not, "Let patience have its perfect work that you might mature in a weak area God wants to target," or "That you might learn the lesson God has been trying to teach you for years." Instead, trials produce patience which leads to maturity that impacts all areas of our Christian lives. The words "perfect," "complete," and "lacking nothing," are all encompassing. Every part of us is affected. If that were not the case, we would not be perfect or complete. We would be lacking.

If I can use a weight lifting analogy, squats are the "King of All Exercises." They receive this title because they train the whole body. Curls train the biceps, bench presses train the chest, pullups train the back, but when you perform squats, you use more muscles than with any other exercise. Trials are like squats because they are difficult and painful, and because they strengthen the entire body spiritually and not just one area. We are always "lacking" on this side of heaven. We never reach "perfection," but trials bring us closer to "completion."

Paul makes this same point in Romans 5:3. First, he says, "We also glory in tribulations," which is similar to "Count it all joy when you fall into various trials" (James 1:2), and "In this you greatly rejoice [when] you have been grieved by trials" (1 Peter 1:6). Then he says: "knowing that tribulation produces perseverance" (Romans 5:3b). The Greek word for "perseverance" is hypomonē, which is the same word for "patience" in James 1:3. Paul says, "Tribulation produces perseverance," and James says, "Trials...produce patience." In the next verse, Paul states what perseverance (or patience) produces: "and perseverance, character; and character, hope" (Romans 5:4). Does patience produce all that? Yes, because trials lead to well-rounded virtue (or maturity) in all areas. There is no godly quality that trials cannot build, and there is no weakness that trials cannot strengthen. In James and Paul's lists, patience is first because it is necessary for other blessings:

- James says patience is the key to being "perfect and complete, lacking nothing" (James 1:4).
- Paul says perseverance (or patience) is the key to "character and hope" (Romans 5:4).

God wants us to learn patience because if we do not, we will learn almost nothing else. William Barclay said:

All kinds of experiences will come to us. There will be tests of sorrows and disappointments. There will be tests of seductions, and tests of dangers, sacrifices, unpopularity which the Christian life must so often involve. But trials are not meant to make us fall; they are meant to make us soar. They are not meant to defeat us; they are meant to be defeated. They are not meant to make us weaker. They are meant to make us stronger. Therefore we should not bemoan trials; we should rejoice in them. The Christian is like the athlete. The heavier the course of training he undergoes, the more he is glad, because he knows that it is fitting him all the better for victorious effort.[12]

Patience and Maturity Go Hand-In-Hand

Consider that a patient person is usually mature, and a mature person is usually patient. Conversely, an impatient person is usually immature, and an immature person is usually impatient. Children are a good example. When we see children throwing a fit because they are not getting what they want, we think, "That is an immature child." When we see children waiting patiently, we think, "That is a mature child." This is why some patient children are more like adults, and some impatient adults are more like children. Maturity is not an issue of age. We reveal our maturity many ways—through our behavior when we do not get what we want, the way we treat those who mistreat us, and the way we respond to trials. These revelations of maturity are related to patience.

What do we teach our children from an early age so they can learn what we want to instill in them? A simpler way to ask this question is: What is the first word we teach our children? "No!" This teaches them one thing: patience. Children are born impatient. They are selfish in that they only think about themselves. We train them to be patient, and as we do, they mature. Parents recognize if their children learn patience, it will go far in helping them excel. The opposite is also true. When children do not learn patience, it negatively affects the rest of their lives.

The Stanford Marshmallow Experiment was a series of studies conducted on children. They were given one marshmallow they could eat immediately, but if they waited until the person conducting the experiment returned about fifteen minutes later, they would receive a second marshmallow. The children fell into two categories—those who ate immediately and those who waited. In follow-up studies conducted years later, the researchers found the children who waited tended to have "better life outcomes as measured by SAT scores, educational attainment, body mass index, and other life measures."[13] Their patience, or impatience, dramatically affected their futures.

God Brings Us into the Deep End

Sermons and books can teach the benefits of patience and how it is acquired, but only trials can build patience into a person's life. Over the last few years, I have been taking my children to the pool to teach them to swim. I can talk about swimming with my children, tell them what it is like, or even show them videos of people swimming. If they are going to learn to swim though, at some point, they must get in the water. The same is true with patience. If we want to learn patience, at some point, we must be immersed in trials.

When I first brought the kids to the pool, I could barely get them down the steps. When I got them down the steps, they stayed glued to the sides. When I got them away from the sides, they did not want to learn to swim. When they learned to swim, they did not want to go in the deep end. I had to repeatedly force them to do things they did not want to do.

The first time I took my oldest child, Rhea, to the deep end, she was terrified. She clung to the side while I talked to her about what I wanted her to do and why I wanted her to do it. She cried and begged me to let her go back to the shallow end. Although I had seen the kids' reluctance since bringing them to the pool, this was the first time I saw genuine fear. I told Rhea, "I have been pushing you since our first visit to the pool. Each time I have had you do things you did not want to do. I know you have not liked it, but if this were not the case you would still be sitting on the steps." Rhea ended up swimming across the deep end. Soon after she began jumping off the diving board and going down the slide. This has been the pattern with each of my children.

Trials are the deep end of the pool. We do not like them. We do not want to be in them. We would rather sit on the steps where we are comfortable and do not have to be challenged or afraid. If we could, we would probably spend our lives in the shallow end, but there would be two unfortunate consequences. First, we would not be much use to God. He cannot do much with Christians who "cannot swim." Second, we would not be much like Jesus.

What does it mean to be "perfect and complete, lacking nothing"? The simplest answer is it means becoming like Christ. God uses trials to conform us into the image and likeness of His Son. This involves removing areas of our lives that keep us from being like Him, and trials accomplish this better than almost anything else. Douglas Kelly said: "As God's dear children, we, who are by grace adopted, are called into the fellowship of suffering, soon enough to be followed by stupendous glory, with the only begotten Son the suffering precedes the glory; the cross precedes the crown, both in the order of experience of the eternal Son of God and also in that of adopted sons and daughters of God." [14]

Perspective Determines
Our Response to Trials

Trials are opportunities for joy, but only opportunities. There is no guarantee we will view them the way God commands. A wrong perspective will prevent us from finding joy in trials.

If we value comfort more than character, then trials will upset us, but if we value maturity more than ease, then we can "count it all joy." God has a greater purpose than our temporary happiness. He is more concerned about us eternally than temporarily. If we live for the physical—the here and now—then we will despise trials. They will make us resentful. Although, if we live for the spiritual—the eternal—then we can embrace trials.

First Peter 1:6 says, "In this you greatly rejoice, though now *for a little while*, if need be, you have been grieved by various trials." Why does Peter say, "for a little while," when a trial can last for years? Because, if we have an eternal perspective, no matter how long any trial lasts, it always looks like "a little while."

Second Corinthians 4:17 says, "For our light affliction, which is but *for a moment*, is working for us a far more exceeding and *eternal* weight of glory." When we consider our afflictions with an eternal perspective, they only last "for a moment." In the next verse, Paul tells us how to have the perspective that is needed during trials: "while we do not look at the things which are seen (an earthly, temporal perspective), but at the things which are not seen (a heavenly, eternal perspective). For the things which are seen are temporary (a little while, for a moment), but the things which are not seen are eternal."

Why Jesus Could Face the Cross with Joy

Although we might be encouraged by the way others handled trials, nobody has ever experienced a trial as well as Jesus. He is our example. God the Son obeyed God the Father perfectly. Jesus did whatever Scripture commanded, including fulfilling the words of James 1:2 decades before they were written. He "counted it all joy" when going to the cross, which was the greatest trial ever experienced. Hebrews 12:2 describes His joy. Let's break up the verse into parts:

- *"Looking unto Jesus"*—He models how to handle trials, so we should set our eyes on Him.
- *"The author and finisher of our faith"*—He allows our faith to persevere through the trials we face.

- *"Who for the joy that was set before Him endured the cross, despising the shame, and has sat down at the right hand of the throne of God"*—Jesus viewed going to the cross with joy, but the cross itself brought Jesus no more joy than the trials we face bring us joy. Our joy comes from knowing what the trials produce, and Jesus' joy came from knowing what the cross would produce.

What did the cross accomplish that was so wonderful to Jesus He experienced something so horrific with joy? It was the joy of knowing our sins would be paid for, redeeming us from the pit of hell, and then He would spend eternity with us. If you have repented and put your faith in Christ, then He endured the punishment your sins deserve. What does it mean to repent and put your faith in Jesus? It means turning from your sins and believing that Jesus is the Son of God who died, was buried, and rose again. If you have not repented and put your faith in Christ, then He has not endured the punishment your sins deserve, and you will have to endure that punishment yourself.

Just as Jesus could view the cross with joy by considering what it accomplished, so can we view trials with joy by considering what they accomplish. When we recognize trials work for us and not against us, then we can face them with joy. God's desire is never to defeat us through trials, whether they be large or small. He brings them to strengthen us. John MacArthur said, "God will always use testing to produce good in us when we meet the test in His power." [15]

Questions

1. How do we demonstrate patience during trials that allows others to see Christ in us?

2. How do you typically respond to trials? Is your reaction based on your earthly comforts or heavenly gain?

3. Discuss three trials in your life and how God used them to help produce patience, mature you, shape your character, and/or strengthen your faith.

    A.

    B.

    C.

4. Discuss three trials you would describe as "God bringing you into the deep end." In other words, they stretched, scared, and/or challenged you.

    A.

    B.

    C.

5. Like Christ, what can you do to focus "on the joy set before you" as you endure trials? In other words, what can you do to "count it all joy" when enduring trials?

6. How do trials help us become more like Christ?

Chapter Four

"Let" Trials Make You Better Instead of Bitter

Looking carefully lest anyone fall short of the grace of
God; lest any root of bitterness springing up cause
trouble, and by this many become defiled.
—Hebrews 12:15

James 1:3b–4 reads, "…the testing of your faith produces patience. But let patience have its perfect work, that you may be perfect and complete, lacking nothing." The wording is odd! If we never read the verses before we would probably expect them to say, "…the testing of your faith produces patience, *which* makes you perfect…" Instead, there are instructive words: "*let* patience have its perfect work." The Greek word for let is *echō,* and it is a verb because James is commanding us to do something. We must "let" trials "work." Echō means, "To have, hold, own, possess, lay hold of."[16] Here are two places it is used:

- Matthew 3:13–14—"Then Jesus came from Galilee to John at the Jordan to be baptized by him. And John tried to prevent Him, saying, 'I need (echō) to be baptized by You, and are You coming to me?'"
- Acts 2:44–45—"Now all who believed were together, and had (echō) all things in common, and sold their possessions and goods, and divided them among all, as anyone had (echō) need."

Of the 712 times echō occurs in the New Testament, 613 times it is translated as "have," because it is not simply about accepting trials in our lives. We must take ownership of them. Instead of resisting trials, we must embrace them. This is how we "let" God use them for our benefit. The alternative is to fight against trials, which hinders the "perfect work" they can accomplish.

Before doctors administer a shot, they say, "Relax. Try to remain as calm as possible. This will hurt, but it will be worse if you resist." The doctor is telling you to accept what is about to happen because failing to do so will only make an already painful situation even worse. It is the same with trials. We cannot avoid them. They hurt, and we make them worse when we resist. Instead, we must accept them, trusting God wants to use them for our good and His glory. This is how we "let" trials make us better.

The Temptation during Trials

Trials and temptations are not the same. Trials are tests from God, and He uses them for our benefit. Temptations, on the other hand, come from our flesh. James 1:13–14 records, "Let no one say when he is tempted, "I am tempted by God"; for God cannot be tempted by evil, *nor does He Himself tempt anyone*. But each one is tempted when he is drawn away by *his own desires and enticed*." As much as God uses trials to bring out the best in us, Satan uses temptations to bring out the worst in us. John Broger said:

> Every person in the world will encounter various trials throughout life. Satan seeks to defeat you by tempting you to trust your own wisdom, to live according to your self-centered feelings, and to gratify the desires of your flesh. In contrast, God's will is for you to be an overwhelming conqueror in all of these tests for His honor and glory.[17]

Although trials and temptations are different for each person, there is one common temptation everyone faces. Even though God uses trials for our good, it is still tempting to become angry with Him. When people are suffering, there is greater potential for them to question, criticize—or worst of all—turn from God. I would love to say, "Trials *always* produce patience, and patience makes you perfect and complete, lacking nothing," but sometimes it would be more accurate to say, "Trials produce bitterness." Perhaps you can think of people experiencing a trial and they said something like, "How could God let this happen to me? I do not deserve it! I wish I could give Him a piece of my mind!" If we are honest, we can probably think of times trials did not produce patience or maturity in us. Instead of making us better, they made us bitter.

Although there are many sins in Scripture, there is no root of lying, stealing, or adultery. Why does Hebrews 12:15 discuss a "root of bitterness?" Roots grow down deep and become difficult to remove, which is also the case with bitterness. Roots can be destructive, ruining sidewalks and the foundations of buildings. Similarly, bitterness can be destructive, ruining relationships in families, work-places, and churches. When people experience trials, especially particularly difficult ones such as a disease or the loss of a child, they might feel betrayed by God. Bitterness can come on quickly, "springing up" as the author of Hebrews warned.

Revelation 3:10 calls the Tribulation "the *hour of trial* which shall come upon the whole world, *to test those* who dwell on the earth." Everyone falls into one of two categories when the trials test them. One group gets better: "Seven thousand people were killed, and the rest were afraid and *gave glory to the God of heaven*" (Revelation 11:13b). Another group gets bitter:

The fourth angel poured out his bowl on the sun...men were scorched with great heat, and *they blasphemed the name of God...they did not repent and give Him glory.* Then the fifth angel poured out his bowl

[and there was] darkness; and they gnawed their
tongues because of the pain. *They blasphemed the God
of heaven* because of their pains and their sores, and
did not repent. Great hail from heaven fell upon
men...*Men blasphemed God* because of the...hail (Revelation 16:8–11, 21).

Both groups experience the same trials, but they produce two different responses. One group is drawn to God.
They "let" trials have their perfect work, and it makes them
better. The other group blasphemes God. They reject the
trials, and it makes them bitter.

A Christian friend's home burned down. His wife and
children were okay, but most of their possessions and
memories were lost. He and his family have served the
Lord faithfully for years. Some people in his situation
would criticize God, wondering why He let something like
this happen to them: "We do not deserve this! What about
everything we have done for You!" The first time I spoke
to my friend after the fire I told him how sorry I was, and
his response was, "Scott, it is just stuff." Not a hint of bitterness. This is the response we need.

In the Hands of the Potter

Since God is sovereign, including over the trials we experience, to reject trials is to reject His will for us. Jeremiah
18:1–3 records an object lesson God used to teach this
truth to His people: "The word which came to Jeremiah

from the LORD, saying: 'Arise and go down to the potter's house, and there I will cause you to hear My words.' Then I went down to the potter's house, and there he was, making something at the wheel." More than likely Jeremiah had passed the potter's house many times in his lifetime, but now God told him to pay a visit. Isaiah 64:8b says, "We are the clay, and You our potter; and all we are the work of Your hand." As Jeremiah watched the potter work, he learned how we should respond to God's work in our lives.

In 2 Corinthians 4:7 Paul called us "earthen vessels." This is fitting since God "formed [us] of the dust of the ground" (Genesis 2:7a). When experiencing trials, probably more than any other time, we recognize the fragile nature of our "clay" bodies. Job especially noticed this during his suffering. He said, "Remember, I pray, that *You have made me like clay*. And will You turn me into dust again?" (Job 10:9; see also Job 4:19).

Job asked God to consider how weak his body was, in the hope it would lead Him to ease his trials. We can feel like this during trials too, wondering if God is aware of our feebleness: "Does He know how weak I am, and that this suffering feels like more than I can handle?" As this account reveals, the Potter is completely familiar with the clay, and He knows best how to handle it.

Clay is a cheap material that remains worthless until it is in the hands of a skillful potter who can make it into something valuable. J. Wilbur Chapman said, "The clay is not attractive in itself, but when the hands of the potter touch it, and the thought of the potter is brought to bear upon it, and the plan of the potter is worked out in it and through it, then there is a real transformation."[18]

The potter sat before two parallel stone wheels joined by a shaft. He turned the bottom wheel with his feet and worked the clay on the top wheel. The clay sat on the wheel as it turned around and around, picturing the way our lives feel at times. Solomon described the repetitiveness: "That which has been is what will be, that which is done is what will be done, and there is nothing new under the sun" (Ecclesiastes 1:9). The potter controls the wheel like God controls the circumstances of our lives. Jeremiah 18:4–6 records:

> And the vessel that he made of clay was marred in the hand of the potter; so he made it again into another vessel, as it seemed good to the potter to make. Then the word of the LORD came to me, saying: "O house of Israel, can I not do with you as this potter?" says the LORD. "Look, as the clay is in the potter's hand, so are you in My hand, O house of Israel!

The Old Testament was primarily written in Hebrew, and the word for "marred" is *shachath*. It means "destroyed or corrupted."[19] It is the same word for "ruin" in Jeremiah 13:7 that describes the sash that was "profitable for nothing." Since clay was cheap, when a vessel was marred or ruined, potters threw it out and started over.

Although, the potter Jeremiah watched worked patiently on the same piece of clay until it became a vessel that "seemed good to [him]." Paul said we can be "confident of this very thing, that He who has begun a good work in you will complete it until the day of Jesus Christ "(Philippians 1:6). We might feel marred, disfigured, or flawed, but instead of discarding us, God can reshape us "into another vessel" that is precious and valuable.

The Hebrew word for potter is *yatsar*, and over half the times it occurs in the Old Testament, it is translated as "form," "fashion," or "make."[20] For example, it is the word God used when commissioning Jeremiah: "Before I formed (yatsar) you in the womb I knew you" (Jeremiah 1:5). As God formed Jeremiah, He will form our lives. As the potter had power over the clay, so God has power over our circumstances. Vessels have a purpose, and God fashions us to fulfill our purpose since "we are His workmanship" (Ephesians 2:10).

The potter's hands shaped the clay, and there are many "hands" God uses to shape us. Parents, siblings, teachers, elders, and authors might come to mind, but Scripture identifies trials as the clearest way God molds us. Unlike the clay on the wheel, which has no free will of its own, we choose how we respond in the Potter's hands. If we are like the clay—soft, pliable, and submissive—then we become better. God will make us into something that "[seems] good to [Him]."

The difficulty is being shaped on the wheel of life is often painful. Trials can tempt us to become bitter toward the Potter who is shaping us. We can become stiff and hard in His hands, which is why Isaiah 45:9 warns:

Woe to him who strives with his Maker! Let the potsherd strive with the potsherds of the earth! Shall the clay say to him who forms it, "What are you making?" Or shall your handiwork say, "He has no hands"?

When we fight against our circumstances, we are fighting against our Maker. Pharaoh demonstrates the painful consequences. Pharaoh hardened his heart the first six times (Exodus 7:13, 22, 8:15, 19, 32, 9:7), God hardened it once (Exodus 9:12), Pharaoh hardened it twice (Exodus 9:34–35), and finally God hardened it five times in a row (Exodus 10:1, 20, 27, 11:10, 14:8). Although Pharaoh first hardened himself, God hardened him by his wishes. This is a sobering example that should encourage us to have soft, teachable, submissive hearts toward the Potter.

When clay becomes as hard as Pharaoh, it can no longer be formed. Then it is good for nothing and must be thrown out. This happened with the Jews. Jeremiah 17:23 says, "But they did not obey nor incline their ear, but *made their neck stiff*, that they might not hear nor receive instruction." The Jews' hardness in chapter 17 led to the command in chapter 18 for Jeremiah to go to the potter's house. God wanted to show His people He was working for their good. They remained hardened though, so then God showed them what happens to stubborn clay.

In the following chapter, God told Jeremiah, "Go and get a potter's earthen flask, and take some of the elders of the people and some of the elders of the priests…Then you shall break the flask in the sight of the men who go with you" (Jeremiah 19:1, 10). God told Jeremiah to bring these leaders with him because this was another object lesson and they could report back to the people what was in store for them if they remained hardened toward God. They would be broken like the clay vessel was broken.

Judas serves as a tragic example of such a broken vessel. Matthew 27:3–7 records:

> Then Judas, His betrayer, seeing that He had been condemned, was remorseful and brought back the thirty pieces of silver to the chief priests and elders, saying, "I have sinned by betraying innocent blood."
> And they said, "What is that to us? You see to it!"
> Then he threw down the pieces of silver in the temple and departed, and *went and hanged himself.*
> But the chief priests took the silver pieces and said, "It is not lawful to put them into the treasury, because they are the price of blood." And they consulted together and *bought with them the potter's field*, to bury strangers in.

The religious leaders used the money to purchase a field where a potter discarded worthless vessels. Judas was overcome with guilt, but instead of trusting God's forgiveness, he committed suicide. Acts 1:18 says he, "purchased a field with the wages of iniquity; and falling headlong, *he burst open in the middle and all his entrails gushed out."* Judas did not purchase the field himself, but since the religious leaders used the money he gave them, it is attributed to him. When Judas hanged himself, either the branch or the rope broke, and his body fell to the ground. The verse creates the image of a vessel being discarded and then breaking open in the field. God did not discard Judas though. Judas discarded himself. Since the field was purchased with Jesus' blood money, it reveals Christ's death has the power to redeem all broken, worthless, and discarded vessels. Judas could have been one of them if he had repented.

These accounts—Jeremiah at the potter's house, Pharaoh, and Judas—are fascinating, because they deal with God's sovereignty and the free moral agency of man. Is the Potter or the clay responsible for the way a vessel turns out?

- In Romans 9:19–21, the Potter looks responsible: "You will say to me then, 'Why does He still find fault? For who has resisted His will?' But indeed, O man, who are you to reply against God? Will the thing formed say to him who formed it, 'Why have you made me like this?' *Does not the potter have power over the clay, from the same lump to make one vessel for honor and another for dishonor?*"

- In 2 Timothy 2:20–21, the clay looks responsible: "In a great house there are not only vessels of gold and silver, but also of wood and clay, some for honor and some for dishonor. Therefore *if anyone cleanses himself from the latter, he will be a vessel for honor,* sanctified and useful for the Master, prepared for every good work."

What is the answer? The correct balance is that while God is sovereign over the trials that come into our lives, we choose how to respond to them. We are in the Potter's hands, and we face two choices:

- If we are soft and pliable, we can become better.
- If we are stubborn and stiff, we can become bitter.

Two individuals in the Old Testament serve as good examples.

David—Made Better by Trials

One of the lowest points in David's life occurred when his son, Absalom, stole the throne from him. Second Samuel 15:13–14 records:

> Now a messenger came to David, saying, "The hearts of the men of Israel are with Absalom." So David said to all his servants who were with him at Jerusalem, "Arise, and let us flee, or we shall not escape from Absalom. Make haste to depart, lest he overtake us suddenly and bring disaster upon us, and strike the city with the edge of the sword."

This had to be excruciating news for David to receive. It was one thing for Absalom to steal the throne, but it was another thing entirely to learn that the Israelites rejected him to embrace his evil son. As a result, David was forced to flee the capital. When things seemed like they could not get worse, Shimei showed up. Second Samuel 16:5–8 says:

> Now when King David came to Bahurim, there was a man from the family of the house of Saul, whose name was Shimei the son of Gera, coming from there. He came out, cursing continuously as he came. And he threw stones at David and at all the servants of King David. And all the people and all the mighty men were on his right hand and on his left. Also Shimei said thus when he cursed: "Come out! Come out! You bloodthirsty man, you rogue! The LORD has brought upon you all the blood of the house of Saul, in whose place you have reigned; and the LORD has delivered the kingdom into the hand of Absalom your son. So now you are caught in your own evil, because you are a bloodthirsty man!"

Since Shimei was related to Saul, he hated David for being king instead of one of Saul's sons. Either he did not know God rejected Saul or he ignored that fact. He also blamed David for Saul's death and the deaths of those in Saul's family, even though David spared Saul's life on multiple occasions and prevented his men from harming him. David's kindness was shown again when his nephew, Abishai, sought to murder Shimei. Second Samuel 16:9–12 records:

[Abishai said,] "Why should this dead dog curse my lord the king? Please, let me go over and take off his head!"

[David replied], "What have I to do with you, you sons of Zeruiah? So let him curse, because *the LORD has said to him, 'Curse David.'* Who then shall say, 'Why have you done so?' See how my son who came from my own body seeks my life. How much more now may this Benjamite? Let him alone, and *let him curse; for so the LORD has ordered him.* It may be that the LORD will look on my affliction, and that the LORD will repay me with good for his cursing this day."

Twice David attributed Shimei's actions to God. There is no indication that God told Shimei to curse David, but it still serves as a powerful example of David's confidence in God's sovereignty. David determined to accept this trial as though it was from God, and there is not a hint of bitterness.

David showed further restraint toward Shimei despite his continued mistreatment: "And as David and his men went along the road, Shimei went along the hillside opposite him and cursed as he went, threw stones at him and kicked up dust. Now the king and all the people who were with him became weary; so they refreshed themselves there" (2 Samuel 16:13–14). How much patience did it take to walk along while Shimei behaved this way? This is what it looks like to surrender to a trial—letting it have its perfect work—so it makes you better.

Asa—Made Bitter by Trials

We discussed Asa, king of Judah, in chapter 1. Second Chronicles 14:2 says he "did what was good and right in the eyes of the LORD his God." He was one of the best kings in the Old Testament. It is important to know that because if trials could make him bitter, we must all be on guard against the same thing happening to us.

Asa was attacked by the northern kingdom of Israel toward the end of his reign. He turned to the king of Syria for help instead of turning to God as he had done when the Ethiopians attacked. He removed silver and gold from the temple to pay for Syria's support. They chased away the Israelites, so it appeared Asa's plan worked. God was displeased with Asa though, and He sent a prophet to rebuke him. Part of 2 Chronicles 16:7–10 records:

> The prophet Hanani said to Asa: "Were the Ethiopians... not a huge army with many chariots and horsemen? Yet, because you relied on the LORD, He delivered them into your hand. In [relying on the king of Syria] you have done foolishly; therefore from now on you shall have wars." *Then Asa was angry with the seer, and put him in prison, for he was enraged at him because of this. And Asa oppressed some of the people at that time.*

Sadly, Asa was so angry, not only did he punish the prophet who rebuked him, he even lashed out at his people. Second Chronicles 16:12 says: "And in the thirty-ninth year of his reign, Asa became diseased in his feet, and his malady was severe; yet in his disease *he did not seek the LORD, but the physicians*." Asa probably had gout or gangrene. Since he reigned forty-one years, this was within two years of the end of his life.

This once great king was on the verge of finishing poorly. Perhaps it is because he had been faithful to God throughout his life that God was still gracious to him despite his sinfulness. What graciousness? This trial (the disease) gave Asa another chance to turn back to God. Unfortunately, Asa failed. There is nothing wrong with turning to physicians for help, but the verse is worded as a criticism of Asa for turning only to the physicians.

Every trial is an opportunity to move closer to God or further from Him. When suffering, we need to ask ourselves:

- Am I letting patience have its perfect work? Am I soft, pliable clay? Am I responding like David? Am I accepting the trials in my life so they make me better?
- Am I preventing patience from having its perfect work? Am I stubborn and stiff in the Potter's hands? Am I responding like Asa? Am I letting trials make me bitter?

Questions

1. Discuss three times you became bitter, or were severely tempted to become bitter, toward God during a trial.

   A.

   B.

   C.

2. What does it mean to "embrace" a trial?

3. In what ways have you turned from God when you experienced a trial?

4. What is the common temptation we face during trials, and why do we face it?

5. How would you recognize if you had "a root of bitterness?"

6. Can you think of other examples in Scripture of people who became better during trials? What about bitter?

Chapter Five

More Precious Than Gold

Examine me, O LORD, and prove me;
Try my mind and my heart.
—Psalm 26:2

I used to be a school teacher, and now I am a pastor. Both professions involve instructing others. I do not want to sound overly simple, but good teachers provide information people do not already have. If they already knew it, they would not need the instruction! Most letters in the New Testament are instructive. There is the occasional time an epistle will say, "I want to remind you..." but primarily they were written to provide new information. This is why James 1:3 is so unique! In the ESV and NIV it says, "*You know that* the testing of your faith produces [patience]." James was not teaching something new. He was telling readers what they already understand about trials. They test our faith!

There are weaknesses with the English language. One weakness relates to the word "know." For example, I use the same English word when I say, "I know my dad" as when I say, "I know of Abraham Lincoln." Obviously, I know my dad much differently than I know President Lincoln. We add the word "of" to differentiate between the types of knowing: knowing someone versus knowing *of* someone.

The Greek word for "knowing of" is *epistamai*. It means, "To put one's attention on, fix one's thoughts on, be acquainted with."[21] This is knowledge, but with no personal interaction or relationship.

The Greek word for "knowing" personally is *ginōskō*, and it means, "to learn to know, get a knowledge of, feel."[22] This is intimate knowledge. Ginōskō is used in Matthew 1:25 to say, "[Joseph] did not know (ginōskō) [Mary] till she had brought forth her firstborn Son." Ginōskō is also the word James uses in verse 3 for "knowing." He tells his readers they know what trials do because they have experienced them before. If you have been through a trial, you also know—they test your faith.

Proving Our Faith

Augustine said, "Trials come to prove us and improve us." This quote identifies the two purposes trials accomplish.

We discussed trials improving (maturing) us. Now we will discuss trials proving our faith.

Let's begin with two other important Greek words. *Peirasmos* is the word for "trials," and it means, "proving, adversity, affliction, trouble sent by God and serving to test or prove one's character, faith, holiness."[23] *Dokimion* is the word for "testing," and it means, "the proving; that by which something is tried or proved, a test."[24] The definitions are similar because trials are tests and tests are trials. Consider the use of both words in James 1:2 and 3: "My brethren, count it all joy when you fall into various trials (peirasmos), knowing that the testing (dokimion) of your faith produces patience." Since the words are similar, the verses could say:

- Count it all joy when you fall into various *trials* knowing the *trying* of your faith.
- Count it all joy when you fall into various *tests* knowing the *testing* of your faith.

Dokimion only occurs one other time, in 1 Peter 1:6–7, which also contains an instance of peirasmos:

In this you *greatly rejoice*, though now for a little while, if need be, you have been grieved by various *trials* (peirasmos), that the *genuineness* (dokimion) of your faith, being much more precious than gold that perishes, though it is tested by fire, may be found to praise, honor, and glory at the revelation of Jesus Christ.

The similarities between James and Peter are strong:

- James says, "count it all joy," and Peter says, "greatly rejoice."
- James says, "[trials] test your faith," and, "Peter says, "[trials] prove the genuineness of your faith."

Peter does not say the genuineness of our faith is precious "like gold." He says it is "much more precious." Why does our faith have this value? We are saved by grace through faith (Ephesians 2:8). Without faith, we have no salvation; therefore, nothing could be more valuable.

Gold is considered a precious metal along with silver, platinum, and palladium. What do people do with these materials? They test them to prove their genuineness. Imagine someone thinks he is holding gold, but it is only pyrite or fool's gold. Imagine a woman thinks her husband bought her an expensive diamond ring, but it is cubic zirconia. John MacArthur said dokimion means, "To put someone or something to the test, with the purpose of discovering the person's nature or the thing's quality."[25] Dokimion was used for coins to determine their value or worthlessness.

If our faith is even more precious than gold, then what will God do with it? As Peter said, He will "[test it] by fire" so "that the genuineness (dokimion) of [it] may be found." In Isaiah 48:10 God said, "Behold, I have refined you, but *not as silver*; I have *tested you in the furnace of affliction*." Our faith cannot be subjected to the same tests as cold metals.

Faith cannot have acid poured on it, receive the scratch test, or be heated to a certain temperature; however, it can be subjected to trials that reveal its value or worthlessness:

- Tom Wells said, "You know why men test gold, why they put it in the fire. They know that if it is gold, fire will not hurt it. Men do not seek to destroy gold with fire. They do not seek to harm it in any way. Instead, they try to prove beyond all doubt that it is gold. And that is what God is doing when He applies [trials]. He seeks to show...that they are true Christians."[26]

- Thomas Kempis said, "Adversities do not make a man frail. They show what sort of man he is."[27]

When trials test us, our faith is at stake. When we pass the tests, we prove the genuineness of our faith. The question is: to whom?

Trials Prove the Genuineness of Our Faith to Us

As already discussed, we should expect trials. This is the case for believers and unbelievers alike. Even the ungodliest people survive some of these trials, and even the godliest people do not always survive trials. For example, cancer is a trial some unbelievers have survived, while some believers have not. This shows surviving (or not surviving) trials does not distinguish Christians from non-Christians.

The question is not, "Did they survive trials?" The question is, "Did their faith survive trials?" When our faith survives trials we can be confident in the genuineness of it. Warren Wiersbe said, "In the 'School of Faith' we must have occasional tests, or we will never know where we are spiritually."[28]

We do not want to wonder where we are going to spend eternity. We want assurance that we have saving faith. James 2:18b says, "I will show you my faith by my works." While our works do not save us, they are one of the clearest indicators that our faith is genuine. Another indicator is when our faith has survived trials. Trials are painful, but one reason we can "count it all joy" when experiencing them is they give us confidence in our faith.

George Muller said, "The only way to learn strong faith is to endure great trials. I have learned my faith by standing firm amid severe testing."[29] He learned to trust his faith because of what it withstood. R.C.H. Lenski said, "If we have true faith we ought to be glad to have it tested and proved to be genuine. If I have genuine gold coins I shall welcome any test to which they may be subjected."[30] Trials reveal the condition of our faith. If we are confident in it, we can welcome trials. When our faith passes the test, we can be blessed knowing it is genuine.

Trials Prove the Genuineness of Our Faith to Others

In the Parable of the Soils, the seed represents the Word of God, and the soil represents our hearts:

> Matthew 13:5–6—"Some [of the seed] fell on stony places, where they did not have much earth; and they immediately sprang up because they had no depth of earth. But when the sun was up they were scorched, and because they had no root they withered away."

"Stony places" refer to shallow soil on top of a bedrock layer, where there is not much depth of earth. As a result, when this soil (or heart) receives the seed (or Word of God), it will not establish deep roots. Think of people who receive God's Word enthusiastically—they are excited about their new faith and "immediately [spring] up"—but they do not last. Their faith does not have deep roots. It looks good at first, but trials reveal it was not genuine:

> Matthew 13:20–21—"He who received the seed on stony places, this is he who hears the word and immediately receives it with joy; yet he has no root in himself, but endures only for a while. For *when tribulation or persecution arises* because of the word, immediately he stumbles."

Sadly, we have all seen people like Jesus described— joyful until they experience trials. How many times have you been at church and heard, "Hey, what happened to so-and-so?" Then someone replies, "Oh, they went through this trial, and they have not been back." Without roots, the insincerity of their faith is exposed, and they revert to their lives before the seed fell on their hearts.

First John 2:19 says, "They went out from us, but they were not of us; for if they had been of us, they would have continued with us; but they went out that they might be made manifest, that none of them were of us." Before "they went out" they looked saved. It was only them going out that revealed "they were not of us."

Unbelievers can look like Christians. The church at Sardis was filled with people who appeared to be Christians, but Jesus told them, "I know your works, that you have a name that you are alive, but *you are dead*" (Revelation 3:1). Sardis looked so good it developed a reputation (a name). Observers thought this was a thriving church because of how much it had going on physically (you are alive). Jesus looked at them and knew they were a church of unbelievers—spiritually dead people.

Trials often reveal that people, such as those in Sardis, are unbelievers. Tying together Jesus' words in Matthew 13:6 and 21 reveals that "tribulation or persecution" caused their faith to "wither away." Sometimes people supposedly get saved and those looking on say, "They are so on fire for God!" That might be true, but until their faith survives trials, it is difficult to be confident.

Trudging through the Swamp of Despair

John Bunyan's famous book, *Pilgrim's Progress*, is an allegory, which means the people, objects, and locations are reflections of their names. The main character, Christian, is reading a Book (the Bible) when Evangelist directs him to leave the "City of Destruction" (the world) to go to the Celestial City (heaven). Soon after Christian begins his journey, Pliable (someone easily swayed without commitment) joins him. At first, Christian and Pliable look equally committed, but that quickly changed when they experienced a trial.

We will pick up when Pliable asked Christian about the blessings he could enjoy when they reached their destination:

Pliable: "Come, neighbor Christian, since there are none but us two here, tell me now further, what the things are? And how to be enjoyed, whither we are going?"

Christian: "I can better conceive of them with my mind than speak of them with my tongue: But yet since you are desirous to know, I will read of them in my Book."

Pliable: "And do you think that the words of your book are certainly true?"

Christian: "Yes verily, for it was made by Him that cannot lie."

Pliable: "Well said, what things are they?"

Christian: "There is an endless Kingdom to be inhabited, an everlasting Life to be given us, that we may inhabit that Kingdom forever."

Pliable: "Well said; and what else?"

Christian: "There are crowns of glory to be given us; and garments that will make us shine like the sun in the firmament of Heaven."

Pliable: "This is very pleasant; and what else?"

Christian: "There shall be no more crying, nor sorrow; for He that is Owner of the place will wipe away all tears from our eyes."

Pliable: "And what company shall we have there?"

Christian: "There we shall be with seraphims, and cherubims, creatures that will dazzle your eyes to look on them. There also you shall meet with thousands, and ten thousands that have gone before us to that place; none of them are hurtful but loving and holy, every one walking in the sight of God, and standing in His presence with acceptance for ever. In a word, there we shall see the elders with their golden crowns. There we shall see the holy virgins with their golden harps. There we shall see men, that by the world were cut in pieces, burnt in flames, eaten of beasts, drowned in the seas, for the love that they bare to the Lord of the place; all well, and clothed with immortality, as with a garment."

Pliable: "The Hearing of this is enough to ravish one's heart...my good companion, glad am I to hear of these things; come on, let us mend our pace."

Everything sounded great to Pliable, just like the blessings of Heaven, eternal life, crowns, and glorified bodies sound great to everyone. Pliable was so excited he even told Christian to walk faster! But then...

> Just as they had ended this talk, they drew nigh to a very miry Slough that was in the midst of the plain, and they being heedless, did both fall suddenly into the bog. The name of the Slough was Despond. Here, therefore, they wallowed for a time, being grievously bedaubed with dirt; and...began to sink in the mire.

They reached their first trial—the Slough (swamp) of Despond (despair). The words "they being heedless" mean they did not see this coming, which is similar to James 1:2 saying we "fall into...trials." We unexpectedly experience trials like Christian and Pliable unexpectedly fell into this swamp. The story continues:

> *Pliable*: "Ah! neighbor Christian, where are you now?"
> *Christian*: "Truly, I do not know."

Christian's response captures the way we often feel during trials: "Things are confusing right now. I do not understand what is happening." We might lack understanding, but understanding is not of greatest importance. Of greatest importance is enduring—continuing to push through the mud. Christian did. Pliable did not:

At that Pliable began to be offended, and angrily said to his fellow, "Is this the happiness you have told me all this while of? If we have such ill speed at our first setting out, what may we expect between this and our Journey's end? May I get out again with my Life, you shall possess the brave Country alone for me." And with that he gave a desperate struggle or two, and got off the mire on that side of the Slough which was next to his own house; so away he went, and Christian saw him no more.

In chapter 1, we discussed the frustration people experience when they wrongly believed the Christian life would be free of difficulties. Pliable is a perfect example. He "[begins] to be offended, and angrily" criticizes Christian. His expectation of further trials was correct, and so he abandoned Christian as quickly as he had joined him. Pliable is like the people who show up at church one day—they look like they are along for the journey—but when troubles arise they leave as suddenly as they came. He looked enthusiastic earlier, but the trial revealed his faith was nothing more than a desire for blessings, with no commitment to Christ.

When Christian later met Goodwill (Jesus), Goodwill said, "How sad it is concerning Pliable in that he had such little appreciation of the heavenly glory to come, so much so that he did not consider it worth encountering a few hazards and difficulties to obtain it." This assessment of Pliable is true of everyone who turns back from following

Christ when trials arise. These people are the opposite of the Apostle Paul who said, "For I consider that the sufferings of this present time *are not worthy* to be compared with the glory which shall be revealed in us" (Romans 8:18). Keeping eternal blessings in mind is one of the best ways to stay encouraged during trials. With so little desire for spiritual realities, Pliable quickly found himself discouraged by the physical and ready to depart.

Later Christian spoke about Pliable with his companion, Faithful:

> *Christian*: When I first set out on my pilgrimage, I did have some hope for that man. But now I fear he will perish in the imminent destruction of the City.
> *Faithful*: They are my fears for him as well.

Pliable departed to avoid his present suffering, but just as Goodwill rightly assessed that Pliable did not think of the glory of heaven, he also did not think of the punishment of hell. When people leave the faith because of suffering, little do they realize the trial they are presently enduring is mild compared to the eternal torment they will suffer for abandoning Christ.

One of the great blessings associated with persevering through trials and proving faith to be genuine is the confidence that hell will not have to be endured. Instead, there is the encouragement that comes from the words of Revelation 21:4: "God will wipe away every tear from their eyes; there shall be no more death, nor sorrow, nor crying. There shall be no more pain, for the former things have passed away."

Trials Prove the Genuineness of Our Faith to God

God reveals Himself through the pages of Scripture. He shows His character and the decisions He makes. We see how He deals with people, and one of the most common ways is through testing them. Here are a few examples:

- Exodus 20:20a—"Moses said to the people, "Do not fear; for God has come to *test* you."
- Job 23:10—"He knows the way that I take; When He has *tested* me, I shall come forth as gold."
- Psalm 66:10—"You, O God, have *tested* us."

Why does God test His people? So He can know them! This is made clear in the Old Testament by understanding two Hebrew words. *Nacah* is the Hebrew word for "tested" or "proved," and it means, "To test, try, prove, tempt, assay."[31] *Yada* is the Hebrew word for "know," and it means, "to know,"[32] but, like ginōskō, it is describing intimate knowledge: "Adam knew (yada) his wife, and she conceived and bore a son" (Genesis 4:1). David used both words when asking God to "test" him to "know" his heart:

- Psalm 26:2—"Examine me, O LORD, and prove (nacah) me; Try my mind and my heart."

- Psalm 139:23–24—"Search me, O God, and know (yada) my heart; Try me...see if there is any wicked way in me."

When God tests people, it is not to imply He did not already "know" them. Nacah is also translated as "prove," because when God tests us with trials, He is proving what is in our hearts. John Fawcett said: "Losses and disappointments are the trials of our faith, our patience, and our obedience. When we are in the midst of prosperity, it is difficult to know whether we have a love for God or only for His blessings. It is in the midst of trials that our faith is put to the test."[33]

Consider these accounts that reveal God's testing through trials:

Israel

Moses could not go with Israel into the Promised Land. Deuteronomy contains his final words to the people he loved and led for forty years. In chapter 8, he discussed the difficult time of testing in the wilderness, and why God put Israel through it: "You shall remember that the LORD your God led you all the way these forty years in the wilderness, to humble you and test (nacah) you, to know (yada) what was in your heart" (Deuteronomy 8:2). God tested Israel in the wilderness to know them.

Fast-forward to Israel entering the Promised Land. God left the enemies in Canaan. Why? Again, God wanted to test Israel to know them: "[The Canaanites] were left, that

[God] might test (nacah) Israel [by them] to know (yada) whether they would obey [His] commandments" (Judges 3:4). God tested the Israelites to know (or prove) whether they would obey Him.

Hezekiah

Hezekiah was one of the greatest kings in the Old Testament, but he failed when Babylon sent messengers to visit him. This evil nation was the superpower of the day and Hezekiah pridefully wanted to impress them; therefore, he showed them his nation's wealth. Second Chronicles 32:31 gives spiritual insight into what took place: "Regarding the ambassadors [from] Babylon...God withdrew from [Hezekiah], in order to test (nacah) him, that He might know (yada) all that was in his heart." God tested Hezekiah to know (or prove) what was in his heart.

Abraham

People struggle with God's command for Abraham to sacrifice his son, Isaac. How could God want a father to sacrifice his own son? God did not want Abraham to sacrifice Isaac. We know that because He stopped it from happening. In Genesis 22:11–12a, the Angel of the LORD said, "Abraham, Abraham! Do not lay your hand on the lad, or do anything to him." The repetition of Abraham's name shows the urgency with which God prevented it, and not only was Abraham not to sacrifice Isaac, he was not to "do anything to him."

If God did not want Abraham to sacrifice Isaac, why did He ask him to do it? The answer is revealed at the beginning of the account: "Now it came to pass after these things that God *tested* (nacah) Abraham" (Genesis 22:1). This was always only a test. It was never about Abraham sacrificing Isaac. It was only about whether Abraham *would* sacrifice Isaac.

This is probably the most fitting picture of a test in all of Scripture. Scholars take notice of the first time God uses a word. It is called "The Principle of First Mention," and the idea is when a word occurs for the first time it reveals the truest meaning.[34] Genesis 22:1 is the first time God uses the word nacah. There were more painful tests—such as what Job experienced—but as far as having faith tested, it is hard to imagine anything tougher than Abraham's experience. He is the "Father of Faith" (Romans 4:11–18) and fittingly He faced the premier test of faith. After he passed, God said, "Now I know (yada) that you fear God, since you have not withheld your son, your only son, from Me" (Genesis 22:12b). God knew the courageous man who dared to pick up the knife would not have hesitated to perform the sacrifice.

The account might look foreign to us because God would never command us to sacrifice a child. There is a relationship though—God tested (nacah) Abraham to know (yada) him, and God tests us to know us. When Abraham's faith withstood the test, the Angel said it revealed his fear of God. When our faith withstands tests, it reveals our fear of God, which is "the beginning of wis-dom" (Proverbs 9:10).

Questions

1. Why is it important for God to test our faith?

2. How can it help your perspective of trials to view them as tests, versus viewing them as unfortunate circumstances?

3. Did you previously consider your faith as being "more precious than gold?" How has your view of your faith changed since reading this chapter?

4. Describe hypothetical people who represent the "seed that fell on stony places." What made them look like Christians before the trial? What changes took place during or after the trial that made them look unsaved?

5. When you have experienced a trial and felt tempted to turn back as Pliable did, what truths can you draw from God's Word to encourage yourself?

6. Can you think of other Scriptural examples of people who experienced trials and proved the genuineness of their faith? What about individuals who proved their faith was not genuine?

Chapter Six

Blessed by Persevering

*Blessed is the man who endures [trials][35]; for when he
has been approved, he will receive the crown of life
which the Lord has promised to those who love Him.*
—James 1:12

Indeed we count them blessed who endure.
—James 5:11a

A few years ago I was experiencing a trial, and this is
part of a message one of my heroes, Dave Zumstein,
sent me:

> It may seem glorious to you to be a mighty man lead-
> ing mighty men into battle. I think it is glorious to
> God to see a man quietly, but strongly, striving to
> fight the good fight amidst difficult times. When the

call comes for difficult times, oh that we might be that type of man.

Dave knew I was an Army officer, so he drew upon something I could appreciate—the contrast between physical and spiritual warfare. Yes, from an earthly perspective, little is more impressive than courageously risking your life in battle. Although, from heaven's perspective, little is more impressive than enduring trials in a God-honoring way. I try to remember the above quote during trials, hoping that by God's grace, I might persevere in a way that pleases Him.

To encourage us "when the call comes for difficult times," James 1:12 and 5:11 state that we are blessed when we endure those trials. The Greek word for "endure" is hypomonē, which is the same word for "patience" in James 1:3 and 4. Many Bibles translate "patience" as "perseverance" or "endurance." This is fitting because patience allows believers to endure and enduring requires patience.

If the word "endure" makes you think of tolerating, think instead of the word "persevere" because James is not describing people putting up with trials. He is describing people who persevere during trials. They come through victoriously. They are triumphant and blessed as a result. Some of the blessings, such as maturity, occur in this life. Other blessings occur in the next life when we hear, "Well done, good and faithful servant" (Matthew 25:23).

No Blessing without Enduring

James 1:12 and 5:11 are past tense. Although the NKJV says, "who endure(s)" in both verses, other translations say, "persevered" (NIV), "endured" (NASB), and "remained steadfast" (ESV). All past tense. Why is that? These verses discuss when the trial is over. Even though James 1:2–4, 1:12, and 5:11 are similar, there is an important difference:

- James 1:2–4 discuss what is happening when trials take place—they produce patience, which produces maturity.
- James 1:12 and 5:11 discuss what happens when trials are over—there is blessing for persevering.

Think back to the account with Abraham. After he persevered, Genesis 22:15–17 says:

> Then the Angel of the LORD called to Abraham a second time out of heaven, and said: "By Myself I have sworn, says the LORD, *because you have done this thing, and have not withheld your son, your only son—blessing I will bless you*, and multiplying I will multiply your descendants as the stars of the heaven and as the sand which is on the seashore; and your descendants shall possess the gate of their enemies.

Abraham was blessed after his trial was over. The same took place with Job: "And the LORD restored Job's losses...Indeed the LORD gave Job twice as much as he had before" (Job 42:10). The same took place with King Asa early in his reign when the Ethiopians attacked him and he trusted God. Not only did God give him the victory, he also blessed him with an immense amount of plunder from the battle. Second Chronicles 14:13b–15 records:

> And *they carried away very much spoil.* Then they defeated all the cities around Gerar, for the fear of the LORD came upon them; and *they plundered all the cities*, for there was *exceedingly much spoil* in them. They also attacked the livestock enclosures, and *carried off sheep and camels in abundance*, and returned to Jerusalem.

Similarly, we often receive the blessings God has for us after the trial is over. Although, since the blessing is associated with the trial, without the trial, there is no blessing. We cannot persevere if there is no trial to persevere through. Warren Wiersbe said: "There can be no victories without battles; there can be no peaks without valleys. If you want the blessing, you must be prepared to carry the burden and fight the battle."[36] Imagine a student who says, "I want to be smart, but I do not want to study," or an athlete who says, "I want to win, but I do not want to practice," or a business owner who says, "I want to make money, but I do not want to work hard." In the Christian life, it is equally foolish to say, "I want a blessing, but I do not want to endure. I want a reward, but I do not want to persevere."

Rather than being discouraging, this should be encouraging. This truth helps us welcome trials because we can look forward to the blessings they provide. This is one more reason we can "count it all joy."

The Greatest Blessing Is Eternal Life

James 1:12 says, "...for when he has been approved, he will receive the crown of life..." The NIV and ESV say, "When he has stood the test." We are saved by grace through faith, so if faith is "tested" and "approved" what should be received? Salvation! That is exactly what James 1:12 promises—the "crown of life" is literally "the crown which consists of life." Enduring trials does not save any more than works save, but since it reveals faith is genuine the result is eternal life. James wants his readers to be encouraged that when their faith has persevered, they can look forward to heaven with the Lord. Of all the blessings Christians receive because of their faith, this is the greatest.

The Apostle Peter makes the same point in his companion passage:

> In this you greatly rejoice, though now for a little while, if need be, you have been grieved by various trials, that the genuineness of your faith, being much more precious than gold that perishes, though it is tested by fire, may be found to praise, honor, and glory at the revelation of Jesus Christ...*receiving the*

end of your faith—the salvation of your souls (1 Peter 1:6–7, 9).

The book of Hebrews was written to Jews who were considering abandoning the faith because of the trials they were experiencing. They were instructed if they persevered they would be saved. Hebrews 10:36 says: "You have need of endurance, so that after you have done the will of God, you *may receive the promise*." This is the promise of eternal life.

A Persevering Saint

Since persevering through trials is so important, we need to know what it looks like to do so. Fortunately, Scripture provides an example: "Indeed we count them blessed who endure. You have heard of *the perseverance of Job* and seen the end intended by the Lord—that the Lord is very compassionate and merciful" (James 5:11). How did Job persevere? He persevered the same way everyone perseveres through trials—by maintaining faith in God.

Twice Satan predicted Job would curse God, and at one point Job's wife even told him to do so. The devil said Job was only faithful to God because of the absence of trials and the abundance of blessings in his life. If God added trials and removed the blessings, Satan was sure Job's faith would not persevere:

- Job 1:9–11—"Does Job fear [You] for nothing? Have You not made a hedge around him, around his household, and around all that he has on every side? You have blessed the work of his hands, and his possessions have increased in the land. But stretch out Your hand and touch all that he has, and he will surely curse You to Your face!"

- Job 2:5—"Stretch out Your hand now, and touch his bone and his flesh, and he will surely curse You to Your face!"

Satan is the Accuser, so this is what we expect him to say. Job's wife's words, on the other hand, are shocking: "Do you still hold fast to your integrity? Curse God and die!" (Job 2:9). What a wonderful woman! I have no idea how one of the greatest men in history ended up with her as a wife, but when you read what she said you learn why the devil killed everyone in Job's life, but let her live! She was Satan's servant. Job rebuked her: "You speak as one of the foolish women speaks. Shall we indeed accept good from God, and shall we not accept adversity?" (Job 2:10a). Basically, he said, "As readily as we accept God's blessings, we must also accept the trials."

Job succinctly described what it means to persevere when he said, "Though He slay me, yet *will I trust Him*" (Job 13:15a). He declared that no matter what happened to him, he would maintain his faith in God. What if Job had not persevered? What if he reached the end of his trials without faith in God? Then he would not have received the crown of life. He would have been like Judas who looked like a believer for some time, but then it was revealed he was unsaved. Believers will persevere and unbelievers will not.

Perseverance Does Not Mean Perfection

Comparing ourselves with Job can be discouraging. Who wants to think they must endure trials as well as he did? We should be encouraged when considering Job's perseverance though because he was far from perfect. Trials bring us closer to perfection, which means we are not yet perfect. Sin has affected every part of us, including the way we respond to trials. Job is an example of this.

James 5:11 says, "You have heard of the perseverance (or patience) of Job," but did Job look patient? Did he remain calm, speaking up only to give praise to God? Did he "count it all joy" when experiencing his trials, or did he express frustration and even criticize God regarding his suffering? Consider the following verses.

Job 9:23—"If the scourge slays suddenly, He laughs at the plight of the innocent."

This is a strong accusation. Job said God mocks the pleas of those killed.

Job 21:4—"As for me, is my complaint against man? And if it were, why should I not be impatient?"

Job said his argument was with God and that he had every reason to be upset.

Job 21:9—"The houses [of the wicked] are safe from fear, neither is the rod of God upon them."

Job said God is unjust, because He does not punish evil-doers.

Job 21:17—"How often is the lamp of the wicked put out? How often does their destruction come upon them, the sorrows God distributes in His anger?"

Job said the wicked live long lives and do not experience the suffering that God inflicts on others.

Job 24:12—"The dying groan in the city, and the souls of the wounded cry out; yet God does not charge [those responsible] with wrong."

Job brought two accusations against God. First, he claimed God was unconcerned with people's suffering. Second, he maintained God did not punish those responsible.

Job also became self-righteous. His final speech to his friends oozed with pride as he described his goodness and innocence:

Job 31:35—"Oh, that I had one to hear me! Here is my mark. Oh, that the Almighty would answer me, that my Prosecutor had written a book!"

Job felt so entitled to hear from God that he challenged Him to write out the accusations against him.

Job 31:36—"Surely I would carry [any accusation] on my shoulder, and bind it on me like a crown."

Job thought the accusations against him were so insignificant he would happily wear them for everyone to see.

Job 31:37—"I would declare to Him the number of my steps; like a prince I would approach Him."

Job was so confident in his righteousness that he would tell God everything he had done. When God was on Mount Sinai "the people trembled and stood afar off. Then they said to Moses, 'You speak with us, and we will hear; but let not God speak with us, lest we die.'" (Exodus 20:18b–19). Job on the other hand claimed he would boldly approach God.

Job 31:38–40—"'If my land cries out against me, and its furrows weep together;
If I have eaten its fruit without money, or caused its owners to lose their lives; then let thistles grow instead of wheat, and weeds instead of barley.'
The words of Job are ended."

Job said he was so innocent that even the land he owned could not bring an accusation against him! What did Job's friends say to him after this? Job 32:1 says: "So these three men ceased answering Job *because he was righteous in his own eyes.*" They knew they could say nothing else to Job, because of the way he viewed himself. Luke 18:9 says the religious leaders "trusted in themselves that they were righteous." Job was dangerously close to becoming like them, but God loved him enough He would not let this pride remain in his heart. He questioned Job in chapters 38 and 39, and after that:

> Job 40:3–5—"Then Job answered the LORD and said:
> 'Behold, *I am vile*; what shall I answer You? I lay my hand over my mouth.
> Once I have spoken, but I will not answer; yes, twice, but I will proceed no further.'"

Things have changed considerably from the last time Job spoke. He went from "righteous in his own eyes" to "vile," from declaring his innocence to wishing he would have "[put his] hand over [his] mouth." Job spent much of the book wanting an audience with God, but when that opportunity came, it did not go the way he anticipated.

Maybe we are like Job, and we want an audience with God. Perhaps our suffering has made us feel mistreated, and we want to bring our accusations against God. If we start to feel that way, we should remember this account with Job. If we were given our day in court with God, our experience would be no different than his. We would move from "righteous in our own eyes" to "vile," and from de-claring our innocence to wishing we would have remained silent.

Further supporting this, God asked Job more questions in chapters 40 and 41. Then Job spoke again:

> Job 42:1–6—Then Job answered the LORD and said:
> "I know that You can do everything, and that no purpose of Yours can be withheld from You.
> You asked, 'Who is this who hides counsel without knowledge?' Therefore I have uttered what I did not understand, things too wonderful for me, which I did not know.
> Listen, please, and let me speak; you said, 'I will question you, and you shall answer Me.'
> I have heard of You by the hearing of the ear, but now my eye sees You. Therefore I *abhor* myself, and *repent* in dust and ashes."

Job's example is doubly instructive. First, he provides encouragement. At times he questioned, criticized, and ac-cused, but he was still a persevering saint. This is not meant to promote sin or disrespect toward God, but it demon-strates persevering through trials does not require perfec-tion.

While it is important to read the victories of great men such as Job, Noah, Abraham, and David, it is also im-portant to read about the times they stumbled. Why? So we can look down on them with disgust, and proudly believe we are better than them? Quite the opposite. Every Christian stumbles, and when that happens, we can be encouraged it even happened to the Heroes of the Faith. Trials test our faith and their accounts teach us that being a Christian does not mean passing every test perfectly.

Second, Job felt "vile" and then he "[abhorred]" himself. This produced something wonderful—his repentance. Job's example also teaches that if we sin during a trial we must repent.

The Difference between Stumbling and Falling

Paul asked, "Have [the Jews] *stumbled* that they should *fall?* Certainly not!" (Romans 11:11a). Stumbling is not the same as falling, and we can see the difference between the two by considering two men who had much in common. Who does this describe?

A well-known man received a unique opportunity when Jesus asked him to become one of the twelve disciples. In accepting the invitation, he was able to be with the Son of God day and night. He became a student of the greatest Teacher in history. When Jesus' enemies tried to trap Him with penetrating questions, he heard the profound theological answers. He saw miracles that showed the Messiah's authority over death, nature, demons, and disease. Jesus gave

him some of the same divine power to cast out demons and perform miracles. He witnessed firsthand
Jesus' love, grace, and mercy. After experiencing all
this, he betrayed Jesus in a strong, convincing way
only hours before His crucifixion. Then he felt great
sorrow.

Who is the man? If you say Judas, you are right. If you
say Peter, you are right. There are plenty of similarities between these men, but one crucial difference. Regarding
their faith, Peter stumbled, but Judas fell. Luke 22:31–34
records:

> And the Lord said, "Simon, Simon! Indeed, Satan
> has asked for you, that he may sift you as wheat. But
> I have prayed for you, *that your faith should not fail*; and
> when you have returned to Me, strengthen your
> brethren."
> But [Peter] said to Him, "Lord, I am ready to go with
> You, both to prison and to death."
> Then [Jesus] said, "I tell you, Peter, the rooster shall
> not crow this day before you will deny three times
> that you know Me."

Notice the words, "that your faith should not fail." Jesus knew Peter's faith was about to be tested, so He graciously warned him. He reverted to Peter's former name,
"Simon," to remind him of his old nature, and repeated it
twice to reveal the gravity of the situation. Peter failed to

appreciate Jesus' warning. He responded pridefully, claiming he would not stumble.

Only hours later, Jesus was arrested and Matthew 26:58 says, "Peter followed Him at a distance to the high priest's courtyard. And he went in and sat with the servants to see [what would happen to Jesus]." During this time they spit on Jesus, beat Him, blindfolded Him, and said, "Prophesy! Who is the one who struck You?" (Mark 14:65, Matthew 26:68). Peter kept his distance because he did not want anyone to recognize him, but his plan failed. Matthew 26:69 says while he "sat outside in the courtyard…a servant girl came to him, saying, 'You also were with Jesus of Galilee.'" Peter denied Jesus three times and became so angry and desperate that he "began to curse and swear, saying, 'I do not know the Man!'" (Matthew 26:74 and Mark 14:71).

Peter stumbled when he had the chance to "confess [Jesus] before men" (Luke 12:8). Luke 22:60a–62 records:

> Immediately, while he was still speaking, the rooster crowed. And the Lord turned and looked at Peter. Then Peter remembered the word of the Lord, how He had said to him, "Before the rooster crows, you will deny Me three times." So Peter went out and wept bitterly.

While being ridiculed and beaten, Jesus made eye contact with Peter. We are not told what Peter saw in that brief look from the Lord, but I suspect it produced the lowest point of his life.

About the same time that Peter denied Jesus, Judas returned the money to the religious leaders. Matthew 27:3–4 records:

> Then Judas, His betrayer, seeing that [Jesus] had been condemned [to die], was remorseful and brought back the thirty pieces of silver to the chief priests and elders, saying, "I have sinned by betraying innocent blood."

Judas betrayed Jesus to the religious leaders for money. Peter denied that he knew Jesus to save himself. Is there much difference between betraying Jesus and denying Him? Not really! Scripture does not tell us who felt worse—Peter or Judas. My suspicion is they felt equally terrible, but the difference is in what their sorrow produced.

Judas felt sorry enough to commit suicide. Peter felt sorry enough to repent. Second Corinthians 7:10 says, "For godly sorrow produces repentance leading to salvation, not to be regretted; but the sorrow of the world produces death." Peter was filled with godly sorrow that produced his repentance. Judas was filled with worldly sorrow that produced his death. When Judas and Peter's faith was tested, Peter stumbled, but Judas fell. Stumbling need not be spiritually fatal.

How do you know whether you have stumbled versus fallen? The answer is contained in the previous words Jesus spoke to Peter: "*when you have returned to Me*, strengthen your brethren" (Luke 22:32b). The person who falls does not return to Jesus. The person who only stumbled does return. This is the sign of a true Christian versus an apostate. The famous Scottish preacher Dr. Alexander Whyte said, "The perseverance of the saints is made up of ever new beginnings."[37] God gave new beginnings to Abraham, Moses, David, Jonah, and Peter when they stumbled, and He does the same for us today. Psalm 37:23–24 (NIV) records:

> The LORD makes firm the steps of the one who delights in him; *though he may stumble, he will not fall, for the LORD upholds him with his hand.*

All Christians stumble, but God does not let them fall. The difference between a Peter and a Judas—a backslider and an apostate—is not that one is perfect, and the other is imperfect. Imperfection and stumbling are what they have in common. The difference is that:

- Unbelievers stumble, which results in them falling.
- Believers stumble, but they get up and return to Christ.

Questions

1. How are patience and endurance similar?

2. What do your questions, criticisms, and/or frustrations toward God during trials reveal about your faith?

3. Describe the changes in Job from the beginning of his trials to the end. What good did God produce in him?

4. How can Job's example encourage us?

5. What is the difference between stumbling and falling?

6. Can you think of other examples in Scripture of individuals who stumbled? What about individuals who fell?

Chapter Seven

Longing for Jesus During Trials

I know that my Redeemer lives,
And He shall stand at last on the earth.
—Job 19:25

When Philip recognized Jesus was the Messiah, he told Nathaniel, "We have found Him of whom *Moses in the law, and also the prophets, wrote*—Jesus of Nazareth, the son of Joseph." (John 1:45). The "law and the prophets" is a New Testament way to refer to the Old Testament. Philip understood Jesus was the Messiah, because the Old Testament is about Him. Jesus taught this too:

- Luke 24:27—"Beginning at Moses and all the Prophets, [Jesus] expounded to them in all the Scriptures the things *concerning Himself.*"
- Luke 24:44—"[Jesus said], 'All things must be fulfilled which were written in the Law of Moses and the Prophets and the Psalms *concerning Me.*'"
- Hebrews 10:7—"[Jesus said], 'Behold, I have come—In the volume of the book it is *written of Me.*'"

How is the Old Testament about Jesus? First, there are around 350 prophecies that He fulfilled. Second, He is revealed through shadows:

- Hebrews 10:1—"The law [was only] a shadow of the *good things to come* instead of the true form of these realities" (ESV).
- Colossians 2:16–17—"[A] festival or a new moon or sabbaths [are] a shadow of things to come, but the substance is *of Christ.*"

Shadows provide an idea of what something looks like without completely revealing the object, which is what the Old Testament does with Jesus. Additionally, seeing a shadow is evidence there is something (or in this case Someone) casting it. Nobody looks at the shadow of a tree or car and thinks it is a tree or car because shadows have no substance; they are not the reality. In the language of Hebrews 10:1 and Colossians 2:17, the reality is found in Christ. He is the substance.

Job looked forward in faith to the Messiah coming, just as we look back in faith believing the Messiah has come. Job's words provide some of the greatest revelation in the Old Testament. Centuries later, Jesus revealed Himself to be the reality and substance of those words.

Job longed for the Messiah while he suffered. Just as Job desired Jesus during his trials, we should desire Jesus during our trials.

A Mediator

Job longed for a Person to stand between him and God:

> Job 9:1–2—Then Job answered and said: "Truly I know it is so, But *how can a man be righteous before God?*"

This is one of the most important questions people can ask. In the following verses, he answered his question and explained why "a man [cannot] be righteous before God":

> Job 9:3–4—"If one wished to contend with Him, he could not answer Him one time out of a thousand. God is wise in heart and mighty in strength. Who has hardened himself against Him and prospered?"

Nobody can stand before God and answer His questions. Job learned this the hard way when he was finally given an audience with Him. At the end of the chapter, he explained the problem and necessary solution:

Job 9:32–33—"For He is not a man, as I am, that I may answer Him, and that we should go to court together. Nor is there any mediator between us, who may lay his hand on us both."

Job needed a Mediator to stand between God and him, and 1 Timothy 2:5 says, "For there is one God and one Mediator between God and men, the Man Christ Jesus." The words "lay his hand on us both" refer to bringing people together, which is how it is translated in some Bibles. Job looked for Someone to reconcile him to God, and 2 Corinthians 5:18 says, "God has reconciled us to Himself through Jesus Christ."

Job 9:34—"Let Him (the Mediator) take His (God's) rod away from me, and do not let dread of Him terrify me."

A rod administers punishment, and Job wanted the Mediator to take away his judgment. Isaiah 53:5 says Jesus "was wounded for our transgressions, He was bruised for our iniquities." The Mediator received the punishment our sins deserve.

Job 9:35—"Then I would speak and not fear Him, but it is not so with me."

Job could approach God confidently if the Mediator did what he described, but he knew that had not been done for him. Jesus has done this for us though, so "we have boldness and access [to God] with confidence through faith in [Jesus]" (Ephesians 3:12).

Job longed for the Mediator during his trials, and He is available to us when we suffer. Jesus allows us to "come boldly to the throne of grace, that *we may obtain mercy and find grace to help in time of need*" (Hebrews 4:16).

An Advocate

Job longed for Someone to plead his case:

> Job 16:19—"Surely even now my witness is in heaven, and my evidence is on high."

A witness speaks on behalf of someone else, and that is what Job wanted. He knew there was Someone to testify on his behalf, and he even knew this Person was "in heaven…on high."

> Job 16:20–21—"My friends scorn me; my eyes pour out tears to God. Oh, that one might plead for a man with God, as a man pleads for his neighbor!"

Job lost everything. Even his "friends" became his accusers. It would not be too much to say that he was the loneliest man in the world. In the face of so much desertion and criticism, he wanted someone on his side. He knew there was an Advocate to defend him the way "a man pleads for his neighbor." When Job knew he did not have anyone else, he knew he had this Person.

Even if we feel as though we have lost everything, we "have an Advocate with the Father, Jesus Christ the righteous" (1 John 2:1). When we suffer, He is "at the right hand of God, [making] intercession for us" (Romans 8:34). Like Job during his trials, if we feel as though we do not have anyone or anything else during our trials, we still have Jesus.

A Redeemer

Job longed for Someone to deliver him out of his suffering:

> Job 19:25–27—"For I know that my Redeemer lives, and He shall stand at last on the earth. And after my skin is destroyed, this I know, that in my flesh I shall see God, Whom I shall see for myself, and my eyes shall behold, and not another. How my heart yearns within me!"

Job knew his Redeemer was alive and He would stand on the earth at the end of time. Satan "struck Job with painful boils from the sole of his foot to the crown of his head" (Job 2:7). Job said, "My flesh is caked with worms and dust, my skin is cracked and breaks out afresh" (Job 7:5). His flesh was in terrible shape, but he knew after it was "destroyed," he would "see God in [his] flesh." How could Job see God in his flesh if his flesh was destroyed? He expected to receive a new body, which 1 Corinthians 15:51–53 describes:

> Behold, I tell you a mystery: We shall not all sleep, but *we shall all be changed*—in a moment, in the twinkling of an eye, at the last trumpet. For the trumpet will sound, and the dead will be raised incorruptible, and *we shall be changed*. For *this corruptible* (earthly bodies) *must put on incorruption* (glorified bodies), *and this mortal* (earthly bodies) *must* put on immortality (glorified bodies).

Job said he would see his Redeemer with "[his own] eyes," and he knew this meant "[seeing] God" Himself. Jesus, the Redeemer, is God: "In the beginning was the Word, and the Word was with God, and the Word was God" (John 1:1). Following the Incarnation, Jesus said, "I and My Father are one" (John 10:30). Our flesh will be destroyed, but we too will receive new bodies and see God for ourselves.

Despite Job's suffering, these thoughts were still enough to cause "[his] heart [to] yearn within [him]." He was overwhelmed as he looked forward in faith to being redeemed. Our joy should be even greater considering we have been redeemed: "Knowing that you were not redeemed with corruptible things, like silver or gold, from your aimless conduct received by tradition from your fathers, but with the precious blood of Christ, as of a lamb without blemish and without spot" (1 Peter 1:18–19). Even during the worst trials, the redemptive work of Christ should cause our "hearts to yearn within [us]" for Him.

Finding Peace Longing for Jesus

What about someone not recorded in Scripture—someone who applied the truths of God's Word to his trials? Horatio Spafford (1828 to 1888) was a devout Christian and wealthy Chicago lawyer. He had a thriving legal practice, a beautiful home, a wife, four daughters, and a son. In 1871, at the height of his financial and professional success, Horatio lost his young son to pneumonia. Later that year, the Great Chicago Fire destroyed most of the real estate investments he owned.

Two years later, Horatio wanted to give his wife, daughters, and himself time to recover from the tragedies they experienced. He decided they would take a vacation in England where he could visit his friend D.L. Moody and hear him preach. Horatio was delayed because of business, so he sent his wife and daughters ahead, letting them know he would join them a few days later. His wife traveled with their four daughters: Tanetta was two, Elizabeth was seven, Margaret was nine, and Anna was eleven.

A few days later, on November 22, 1873, Horatio received the news that another vessel struck the ship his wife and daughters were on, and 226 people lost their lives, including Horatio's four daughters.[38] Only his grieving wife survived. Horatio sailed to England to see her, and as he traveled near the location of his daughters' deaths, he was inspired to write the hymn, "It Is Well with My Soul."[39] Part of it reads:

When peace, like a river, attendeth my way,
When sorrows like sea billows roll;
Whatever my lot, Thou hast taught me to say,
It is well, it is well with my soul.

What allowed Horatio to have peace during such an excruciating time? He reflected on the work Christ accomplished for him. Reflecting on the work Christ accomplished for us can give us peace during excruciating times:

Though Satan should buffet, *though trials should come,*
Let this blest assurance control,
That *Christ hath regarded my helpless estate,*
And *hath shed His own blood for my soul.*

My sin—O, the bliss of this glorious thought,
My sin, not in part but the whole,
Is nailed to the cross, and I bear it no more,
Praise the Lord, praise the Lord, O my soul!

Like Job, whose "heart yearned within [him]" as he thought about his Redeemer, so was Horatio overwhelmed by the "glorious thought" of his redemption. Similarly, thinking about our redemption can help us find joy during trials.

As much as Horatio considered what Jesus had done for him in the past, he also thought about seeing Him in the future:

And *Lord, haste the day when the faith shall be sight,*
The clouds be rolled back as a scroll;
The trump shall resound, and *the Lord shall descend,*
Even so, it is well with my soul.

Horatio knew his suffering was temporary and one day he would be with his Savior. Regardless of the trial we experience, reflecting on what Jesus has done for us and looking forward to being with Him can give us peace during our suffering too.

Job—A Type of the True and Greater Intercessor

After Job suffered, he served as one of the clearest types of Christ in the Old Testament. Job longed for his Mediator, Advocate, and Redeemer throughout his trials, and then he became a picture of that Person to his friends. Job 42:7–8 records:

And so it was, after the LORD had spoken these words to Job, that the LORD said to Eliphaz the Temanite, "*My wrath is aroused against you and your two friends,* for you have not spoken of Me what is right, as My servant Job has. Now therefore, *take for yourselves seven bulls and seven rams, go to My servant Job, and offer up for yourselves a burnt offering; and My servant Job shall pray for you. For I will accept him, lest I deal with you according to your* folly; because you have not spoken of Me what is right, as My servant Job has."

How could God's wrath against Job's friends be turned away? This was hundreds of years before the Mosaic law instituted the sacrificial system, but even then it was clear an offering needed to be made for sin. Seven is the number of completion, which means Job's offering pictured a perfect sacrifice on his friends' behalf. God did not treat Job's friends "according to [their] folly," which is to say they did not receive the punishment they deserved. They avoided judgment because of Job's intercession for them. Similarly, God's wrath is against us, but Jesus offered a perfect sacrifice on our behalf. We do not receive the punishment our sins deserve. We avoid judgment, because of Jesus' intercession for us.

Job 42:9 says, "So Eliphaz the Temanite and Bildad the Shuhite and Zophar the Naamathite went and did as the LORD commanded them; for the LORD had *accepted* Job." Job's friends did not accept him, but in verse eight God said, "I will accept [Job]," and now it says God "accepted Job." Those closest to Job rejected him like those closest to Jesus rejected him, but God accepted Job on their behalf like God accepts Jesus on our behalf.

Job 42:11—"Then all his brothers, all his sisters, and all those who had been his acquaintances before, came to him and ate food with him in his house; and they consoled him and comforted him for all the adversity that the LORD had brought upon him. Each one gave him a piece of silver and each a ring of gold."

Job was rejected by his family but then accepted by them, like Jesus was first rejected by his family and then accepted by them. Job experienced suffering and humiliation, but then blessing and exaltation. Jesus experienced suffering and humiliation, but He will experience blessing and exaltation as described in Philippians 2:7–11:

[Jesus] made Himself of no reputation, taking the form of a bondservant, and coming in the likeness of men. And being found in appearance as a man, He humbled Himself and became obedient to the point of death, even the death of the cross. Therefore God also has highly exalted Him and given Him the name which is above every name, that at the name of Jesus every knee should bow, of those in heaven, and of those on earth, and of those under the earth, and that every tongue should confess that Jesus Christ is Lord, to the glory of God the Father.

Job's friends honored him because of what he did for them. How much more honor should we give Christ, because of the greater work He did for us as our Mediator, Advocate, and Redeemer?

Jesus—The Only Innocent, Righteous Sufferer

The first two chapters of the Book of Job contain what could be the greatest description of an individual in all of Scripture, second only to Christ Himself. Job 1:1 says, "There was a man in the land of Uz, whose name was Job; and that man was *blameless and upright*, and *one who feared God and shunned evil.*" When God spoke to Satan about Job, He said, "Have you considered My servant Job, that *there is none like him on the earth, a blameless and upright man, one who fears God and shuns evil?*" (Job 1:8). After Satan destroyed Job's animals, servants, and children, God repeated to Satan what He previously said and added, "Still *he holds fast to his integrity, although you incited Me against him*, to destroy him without cause" (Job 2:3).

Job's description contributes to the main struggle people have with the account. If Job looked like a terrible sinner who "had it coming," there would be no dilemma. Instead, people ask, "How could God let an innocent, righteous man experience such terrible suffering?" Despite Job's character, he was still a sinner: "There is none righteous; no, not one" (Romans 3:10). We saw some ways Job's trials revealed his weaknesses—he criticized God and he was self-righteous.

There has only been one perfectly righteous, innocent Sufferer, and that is Jesus. The Gospels go to great lengths throughout His trials to reveal this:

- Matthew 27:19—Pilate's wife said, "Have nothing to do with *that just Man*."
- Matthew 27:24—Pilate said, "I am innocent of the blood of *this just Person*."
- Luke 23:41—One of the criminals on the cross next to Jesus said, "*This Man has done nothing wrong.*"
- Luke 23:47—The centurion said, "Certainly *this was a righteous Man!*"

Job suffered and then saved his friends, but he looked forward to the Man who suffered and saved His friends in the true and greater sense. Job suffered, but Jesus suffered for the sins of others. Job offered a sacrifice for his friends, but Jesus offered the one sacrifice that provided eternal life: "This Man, after He had offered one sacrifice for sins forever, sat down at the right hand of God" (Hebrews 10:12). Job saved his friends physically and temporarily, but Jesus saves His friends spiritually and eternally.

Questions

1. During trials, how can you be encouraged thinking about the Mediator, Advocate, and Redeemer you have in Jesus?

2. What other roles does the Lord fill that can encourage you during trials? For examples, look at Psalm 18:2, 27:1, and 144:1–2.

3. How can longing for Jesus give you peace during trials?

4. Do you see any other ways Job served as a type of Christ? If so, list them.

5. In what ways is Jesus the true and greater Intercessor, and the only innocent, righteous Sufferer?

6. Can you think of other examples in Scripture of individuals who served as types of Christ during their suffering?

Chapter Eight

The End Intended by
the Lord in Trials

*You have heard of the perseverance of Job and seen
the end intended by the Lord—that the Lord is very
compassionate and merciful.*
—James 5:11b

God does not use highlighting, italics, bold, or under-
lining for emphasis, but He does use repetition.
Twice God told Eliphaz, "you have not spoken of me what
is right, as My servant Job has," and He added that this is
what caused "[His] wrath [to be] aroused against [Job's
friends]" (Job 42:7–8). God does not like to be misrepre-
sented!

When God said Job "[spoke] of [Him] what is right" He
was not referring to Job's words in chapters 3 through 31.

That is when many of Job's statements were incorrect. Instead, God referred to Job's responses in chapters 40 and 42 after He questioned him. That is when Job "spoke of [God] what is right," and God commended him for it before his friends. God wants to be represented correctly.

Remembering God's character is always important, but it is especially important during trials. When suffering, we are tempted to draw incorrect conclusions about God: "God is not good," "God has forgotten about me," "God has changed," or "God does not love me." This is when we must turn to Scripture to be convinced of the truth and see what is "spoken of [God that] is right." What does the Bible say about God's character and actions when we suffer? According to James 5:11 He is "very compassionate and merciful." The Bible contains several accounts that depict God this way:

- Manasseh was the wickedest king in the Old Testament. It seemed like there was no false god he did not worship, and no command he did not break, including going so far as to sacrifice his sons. God punished him by taking him into captivity, and 2 Chronicles 33:12–13 records: "Now when he was in affliction, he implored the LORD his God, and humbled himself greatly before the God of his fathers, and prayed to Him; and *He received his entreaty, heard his supplication, and brought him back to Jerusalem into his kingdom.* Then Manasseh knew that the LORD was

God." God not only forgave Manasseh, He even restored him as king.

- The Ninevites were some of the evilest people in the Old Testament, but when they repented, God spared them. This made Jonah so angry that he wanted to die, but God rebuked him: "*Should I not pity Nineveh, that great city, in which are more than one hundred and twenty thousand persons who cannot discern between their right hand and their left?*" (Jonah 4:11).

- The Parable of the Prodigal Son reveals the heart of God the Father. Luke 15:20 says the son "arose and came to his father. But when he was still a great way off, *his father saw him and had compassion, and ran and fell on his neck and kissed him.*"

- When Jesus was crucified He prayed, "*Father, forgive them,* for they do not know what they do" (Luke 23:34).

These accounts make God look "very compassionate and merciful," but He does not look that way regarding His treatment of Job. If someone said, "Show me an example of God being 'very compassionate and merciful,'" you probably would not point to Job. Trials can make God look unmerciful and cruel. We tend to think if God was compassionate and merciful, He would not let people suffer, but James 5:11 says that even with Job—a man whose very name is associated with trials—God was still "very compassionate and merciful." If God can be described this way with Job, then regardless of our trials, we must recognize God is still acting very compassionately and mercifully toward us.

God's Compassion and Mercy to Job (and Us)

How was God compassionate and merciful toward Job? As already discussed, God blessed him with twice as much as he had before, and vindicated him before his family and friends (Job 42:10–11; see chapters 6 and 7).

Second, God put restrictions on what Satan could do to Job. We might not be comfortable with those restrictions, but they were present nonetheless:

- Job 1:12—"The LORD said to Satan, 'Behold, all that he has is in your power; only do not lay a hand on his person.'"
- Job 2:6—"The LORD said to Satan, 'Behold, he is in your hand, but spare his life.'"

No matter how painful a trial might be—physically, mentally, emotionally, or spiritually—God still restricted it from being worse. As a pastor, I have regularly told people not to say, "It could be worse," but it is true—things could always be worse. If we could see how much worse, we would be thankful for God's compassion and mercy.

Third, although Job was a godly man, we saw he sinned toward God. He was angry, accusing, and demanding. He thought God owed him an audience and explanation. He was self-righteous, especially when declaring his innocence. Even this criticized God, because it implied He was unjust for treating Job so poorly. God revealed His compassion and mercy when He spoke to Job, but did not kill him.

Most parents would not let their children speak to them the way Job spoke of God, but God did little more than ask Job difficult questions he could not answer. While nobody would want to be questioned by God the way Job was, this was mild considering the punishment Job deserved. The lesson is we deserve much worse than we receive. If God gave full vent to His wrath, we would be destroyed. Instead:

- Lamentations 3:22—"*Through the* LORD*'s mercies we are not consumed*, because His compassions fail not."
- Hosea 11:8b–9a—"My heart recoils within me; my compassion grows warm and tender. *I will not execute My burning anger*" (ESV).
- Job 34:14–15—"*If He should set His heart on it*, if He should gather to Himself His Spirit and His breath, all *flesh would perish together, and man would return to dust*."

The final way God was compassionate and merciful to Job is shown by the words "end intended by the Lord" (James 5:11). This phrase is so important you might underline, circle, or highlight it in your Bible. Do whatever you need to do to make sure you do not forget it. These words state that whatever trial we experience, God has a reason for it.

In Job's case, God intended to remove his pride. God might use trials to accomplish the same end in our lives. Few things humble people more effectively than trials. Suffering is an equalizer that can bring even the highest people low.

God also used Job's trials to provide revelation of His Son through the previously discussed words Job spoke. Likewise, God wants to use our trials to reveal His Son. Few times in our lives do we have as much opportunity to bring glory and honor to Christ than when we suffer. Why? Since it is so easy to speak well of the Lord while prospering it is not as meaningful to others. When Christians praise the Lord during the darkest trials, those looking on cannot help but be moved by the Gospel shining through the suffering. First Peter 4:16 says, "Yet if anyone suffers as a Christian, let him not be ashamed, but let him glorify God in this matter."

Regardless of what God is doing, we can be confident He does not allow suffering except for His purpose.

The Good God Brought from Tragedy

My only sibling, Jason, was fourteen months younger than me. Growing up we were similar athletically and academically, but during high school he started partying and abusing drugs. He dropped out of school and received his GED. We were encouraged when Jason enlisted in the

Army and joined the 82nd Airborne, which involved jumping out of planes. He said he developed pain in his knees, but we do not know if that was true or an excuse to obtain prescriptions from the military hospital. Either way, this is when he became addicted to pills.

Jason separated from the Army after four years of service. He started breaking into people's homes and raiding their medicine cabinets to satisfy his addiction. He was arrested and I still remember how difficult it was the first time we visited Jason in jail and had to speak to him on opposite sides of the glass. He was released, but soon after was arrested again. Unable to find a job because of his criminal record, he moved across the country hoping to rejoin the military. That was the last time we saw him. A few months later, I received the phone call from my dad that Jason had overdosed in a motel room.

I was in my early twenties, single, and teaching elementary school at the time. I threw myself into my work, hoping to stay distracted from the grief. It did not work. I was struggling.

A Christian friend who worked with me said, "My pastor lost his brother when he was about your age. You should come to church with me and speak to him. It might make you feel better." I had no intention of becoming a Christian because I thought I was a good person who would go to heaven. The idea of being saved or born again was foreign to me, but going to the church to speak to the pastor was attractive. I had never attended a Christian church before. During the sermon, for the first time in my life, God spoke to me through His Word. Though I did not meet with the pastor about my brother that day, I already looked forward to returning the following Sunday. Soon after, I repented of my sins and put my faith in Christ.

A few years after my conversion, I reconnected with Katie. We were pleasantly surprised to find the other had also become a Christian. Less than a year later, we married. Around the same time, my heart for teaching decreased and my heart to be a pastor increased. I started working part-time as an associate pastor, and when the church grew, they hired me full-time as an associate pastor.

My greatest desire during that season was seeing my parents become Christians too. After praying and sharing the gospel with them for about five years, they surrendered their lives to Christ. Ephesians 3:20 says, "[God] is able to do exceedingly abundantly above all that we ask or think," and this verse was fulfilled in my life when I baptized Mom and Dad. They moved to be with us in central California, and when I received the senior pastor position at Woodland Christian Church, they followed us up to Washington. Dad serves as a deacon in the church, and I dedicated my previous book, *Marriage God's Way*, to him because of the courageous, faith-filled way he has endured his trial with Alzheimer's.

My brother's overdose was the darkest, most painful situation I have experienced, but I can say God brought forth more good from it than any other event in my life. Jason's death led to me visiting a church where I learned the gospel. My salvation, my parents' salvation, the privilege of raising seven children (and possibly more) to serve the Lord, and over ten years of pastoral ministry are a few ways God made "all things work together for good" (Romans 8:28). I could not see it at the time, but I can look back now and recognize the wonderful end intended by the Lord.

We Cannot Always See the End Intended by the Lord

The Book of Job is forty-two chapters long. The first two chapters reveal the conversation between God and Satan that sets in motion the following forty chapters. James 5:11b says, "*You* have heard of the perseverance of Job." Who is "you"? It is us! We can read the discussion between God and Satan to see why Job's suffering took place, but who could not see "the end intended by the Lord"? Job! He experienced trials that did not make sense to him because he had no idea what took place behind the scenes.

Consider Abraham again. Since Genesis 22:1 says, "God tested Abraham," we know it was a test, but who did not have this knowledge? Abraham! All he knew were the words of Genesis 22:2: "Offer [Isaac] as a burnt offering." He had to wonder why God would make this request. He must have struggled with the morality of taking his son's life. Abraham did not hear from God again until Genesis 22:12 when the Angel of the LORD said, "Do not lay your hand on the lad…for now I know that you fear God." At that moment, Abraham learned it was a test, but he did not know that earlier during the three most difficult days of his life.

While Job's trials would have been difficult regardless of his understanding, they would have been more bearable if he had the insight we are given. Much of his frustration during the conversations with his friends came from his confusion. Job's friends said he was a terrible sinner, but God's assessment was: "There is none like [Job] on the earth, a blameless and upright man, one who fears God and shuns evil?" (Job 1:8, 2:3). We know God said this, but Job had no idea. He was forced to wonder, "Are my friends, right? Is God angry with me? Has He forsaken me?" These are the same questions we might ask when suffering.

Even though we are privy to the conversations between God and Satan, we still have questions: "Why would God let Satan do anything to Job? God stopped Satan from doing certain things. Why did He not stop Satan completely?" We do not know. The Bible does not tell us. When some people experience a particularly difficult trial, they feel as though God owes them an explanation. If God did not need to explain Himself to Job—a man who experienced the worst trials imaginable—He does not need to explain Himself to us.

The Need to Trust God

What if Abraham never picked up the knife? Even though he had a long record of obedience, he would not have passed the test. James 2:21 says, "Was not Abraham our father justified by works *when he offered Isaac his son on the altar?*" It does not say "when he walked to Moriah," "when he built the altar," "when he bound Isaac," or even, "when he laid him on the altar." It says, "when he offered Isaac." Does this mean we are "justified (or saved) by works"? No, we are saved by grace through faith (Ephesians 2:8), but when Abraham raised his hand, it proved "the genuineness of [his] faith" (1 Peter 1:7).

Hebrews 11:19 says Abraham "[concluded] that God was able to raise [Isaac] up, even from the dead." Abraham had every intention of sacrificing his son, believing God would bring him back to life: "Abraham said to his young men, 'Stay here with the donkey; the lad and I will go yonder and worship, and *we will come back to you*'" (Genesis 22:5). As confident as Abraham was about walking up the mountain with Isaac, he was equally confident about returning with him.

Why did Abraham have this certainty? God promised him he would have countless descendants through Isaac (Genesis 15:5, 21:12), but Isaac had not had any children when Abraham received the command to sacrifice him. There were only two possibilities—God would raise Isaac from the dead or He would become a liar. Abraham had his answer, because he believed the words of Hebrews 6:18 centuries before they were written: "It is impossible for God to lie." Although Abraham did not know what God was doing, he trusted Him, and that allowed him to persevere. James 2:22 confirms this: "Do you see that *faith was working together with his works*, and by works faith was made perfect?" We might be tempted to applaud Abraham's strength, courage, or determination, but Scripture credits his faith.

We are often in the same situation Job and Abraham found themselves in—we do not know the end intended by the Lord. While I can look back now and see the good God brought from my brother's death, this has not been the case with other trials in my life. Most of the time I have been forced to simply trust God. On this side of heaven "we see dimly [and only] know in part" (1 Corinthians 13:12). As a result, we need to walk by faith like Abraham did. Enduring trials is not an issue of strength, intelligence, or money. Whether trials make sense or seem fair is irrelevant. The only question is, "Will I trust God?"

Questions

1. Which of the four examples of God's compassion and mercy most encouraged you? Why?

2. Can you think of other examples in Scripture of God's compassion and mercy toward individuals during trials?

3. Provide three examples from your life, or the life of others that demonstrate God's compassion and mercy during trials.

    A.

    B.

    C.

4. Since God uses repetition for emphasis, what has He repeated about trials in Scripture? Give three examples.

    A.

    B.

    C.

5. During trials, what characteristics of God can you focus on to help you better endure trials? Write down a verse (or two) to memorize that reveals this characteristic.

6. Job 42:11 says, "All the adversity that *the* LORD *had brought upon him."* How do we reconcile God's goodness, love, compassion, and mercy, with this verse?

7. Unbelievers and some genuine believers ask, "Why would a loving God ____?" How would you answer this question, considering 1 Peter 3:15 says we must "always be ready to give a defense to everyone who asks [for] a reason for the hope that is in" us?

8. When has God used a trial in your life to bring forth good? In other words, when have you been able to look back on a trial and see the end intended by the Lord? Provide two examples.

   A.

   B.

9. When have you had to trust God and walk by faith? Provide two examples.

   A.

   B.

Chapter Nine

The Trials We Endure
Are Supremely About Jesus

But as for you, you meant evil against me; but God
meant it for good, in order to bring it about as it is
this day, to save many people alive.
—Genesis 50:20

When Abraham "sacrificed" Isaac, it was secondarily about an earthly father sacrificing his earthly son. Primarily it foreshadowed God the Father sacrificing His Son. When Job "saved" his friends, it was secondarily about Job and his friends. Primarily it foreshadowed Jesus saving His friends. Abraham and Job's trials were supremely about Jesus. Similarly, our trials are secondarily about us. Supremely they are about Jesus—His glorification is the primary end intended by the Lord. John 11:3–4 records:

Therefore [Lazarus's] sisters sent to [Jesus], saying, "Lord, behold, he whom You love is sick."

When Jesus heard that, He said, "This sickness is not unto death, but for the glory of God, *that the Son of God may be glorified through it.*"

Joseph's Trials—Supremely About Jesus

Genesis 37 records Joseph being rejected by his brothers, thrown into a pit, and then captured by Midianites, but verse two says, "This is the history of Jacob." Why would a chapter about Joseph say it is about Jacob? Jesus came from Jacob instead of Joseph, which puts the focus on Jacob, even though Joseph is discussed. The bigger picture in Genesis 37 is Joseph gets to Egypt. Twenty years later, his family moves to Egypt. Joseph's brothers have enough descendants to become the twelve tribes of Israel. Fast-forward fifteen hundred years, and that nation produces a Savior. Everything Joseph experienced—every trial—was about Jesus. He is revealed through Joseph like He was revealed through Abraham and Job.

> Genesis 37:12–14—"Then [Joseph's] brothers went to feed their father's flock in Shechem. And [Jacob] said to Joseph, 'Are not your brothers feeding the flock in Shechem? Come, I will send you to them.' So he said to him, 'Here I am.'
> Then he said to him, 'Please go and see if it is well with your brothers and well with the flocks, and

bring back word to me.' So he sent him out of the Valley of Hebron, and he went to Shechem."

Joseph's father sent him to his brethren, like Jesus' Father sent Him to His brethren, the Jews. In Matthew 15:24 Jesus said, "I was not sent except to the lost sheep of the house of Israel."

Genesis 37:15–18—"Now a certain man found him, and there he was, wandering in the field. And the man asked him, saying, 'What are you *seeking*?' So he said, 'I am *seeking* my brothers. Please tell me where they are feeding their flocks.' And the man said, 'They have departed from here, for I heard them say, "Let us go to Dothan." So Joseph went after his brothers and found them in Dothan. Now when they saw him afar off, even before he came near them, they conspired against him to kill him."

Notice the repetition of "seeking." Joseph was seeking his lost brethren, revealing the heart of Christ in seeking His lost brethren. Luke 19:10 says, "The Son of Man has come to seek and to save that which was lost."

When Joseph came to his brothers, they would not accept him, and when Jesus came to His brethren, they would not accept Him. John 1:11 says, "He came to His own, and His own did not receive Him."

Genesis 37:19–20—"Then they said to one another, 'Look, this dreamer is coming! Come therefore, let us now kill him and cast him into some pit; and we shall say, 'Some wild beast has devoured him.' We shall see what will become of his dreams!'"

It is hard to put into words the wickedness of Joseph's brothers plotting his death, but even these dark verses beautifully reveal Jesus. John 11:53 says, "Then, from that day on, they plotted to put [Jesus] to death."

Genesis 37:21–22—"But Reuben heard it, and he delivered him out of their hands, and said, 'Let us not kill him.' And Reuben said to them, 'Shed no blood, but cast him into this pit which is in the wilderness, and do not lay a hand on him'—that he might deliver him out of their hands, and bring him back to his father."

Reuben was the oldest, which made him the de facto leader. He knew Joseph was innocent and should not be murdered, so he tried to deliver him out of his brothers' hands. Pilate was the leader of the Jews. He knew Jesus was innocent and should not be murdered, so he tried to deliver Him out of the Jews' hands. The Jews said, "Let Him be crucified!" and Pilate said, "Why, what evil has He done?" (Matthew 27:22–23).

Genesis 37:23—"So it came to pass, when Joseph had come to his brothers, that they stripped Joseph of his tunic, the tunic of many colors that was on him."

Joseph was stripped of his tunic, like Jesus was stripped of His: "Then the soldiers, when they had crucified Jesus, took His garments…and also the tunic. Now the tunic was without seam, woven from the top in one piece" (John 19:23).

Genesis 37:24—"Then they took him and cast him into a pit. And the pit was empty; there was no water in it."

They threw Joseph into the pit to die. In the Old Testament, "the pit" is another name for the grave, so this pictures Christ's death and burial. Psalm 88 is a messianic psalm, which means we can read much of it as though Jesus is speaking. In verse 10, He said, "You have laid me in the lowest pit, in darkness, in the depths."

Genesis 37:25a—"And they sat down to eat a meal."

They threw Joseph into a pit to die while they sat down to eat. It is hard to believe they could treat anyone like this, much less their brother, but again, Christ is revealed. Their indifference toward Joseph resembles the indifference shown to Jesus when He was on the cross: "The chief priests [were] mocking with the scribes and elders" (Matthew 27:41).

Genesis 37:25b–28a—"Then they lifted their eyes and looked, and there was a company of Ishmaelites, coming from Gilead with their camels, bearing spices, balm, and myrrh, on their way to carry them down to Egypt. So Judah said to his brothers, 'What profit is there if we kill our brother and conceal his blood? Come and let us sell him to the Ishmaelites, and let not our hand be upon him, for he is our brother and our flesh.' And his brothers listened. Then Midianite traders passed by; so the brothers pulled Joseph up and lifted him out of the pit."

They did not want to murder Joseph because it would not make them money, so they lifted him out. Since he was in the pit to die, this figuratively pictures his resurrection from the dead. Psalm 16 is another messianic psalm, and in verse 10 Jesus said, "For You will not leave My soul in the pit, nor will You allow Your Holy One to see corruption" Peter quotes this verse in Acts 2:27, and Paul quotes it in Acts 13:35 as prophecies of Jesus' resurrection.

Genesis 37:28b—"[They] sold him to the Ishmaelites for twenty shekels of silver."

Joseph was sold for the price of a slave, and so was Jesus. Exodus 21:32 identifies thirty pieces of silver as the value of a slave, and Matthew 26:15 says, "[Judas] said, 'What are you willing to give me if I deliver Him to you?' And they counted out to him thirty pieces of silver."

Genesis 37:28c—"And they took Joseph to Egypt."

Jesus was also taken to Egypt. Matthew 2:14 says, "[Joseph] took the young Child and His mother by night and departed for Egypt." The account appears tragic, but with the words of Genesis 37:28 we see "the end intended by the Lord." Joseph is in Egypt, which served as the womb for Israel to grow into the nation that produced the Messiah.

Later, Joseph was thrown in prison after being falsely accused by Potiphar's wife. The cupbearer was released from prison, but he "forgot" he promised to help Joseph. Joseph was separated from his family for twenty years, not knowing who was alive or dead.

While Joseph suffered, did he have any idea what God was doing? When he was in the pit or prison, he could not say, "God wants me in Egypt, so I can save the known world from starvation. Later the Messiah, who will deliver the world from sin and death, will come from my descendants. All the while I can serve as a tremendous type of that Savior."

Joseph's trials were made worse by his lack of knowledge. Like Abraham, Job, and us, Joseph was forced to walk by faith. He was blind to what God was doing until the end, but did God have an intended end? He most definitely did, and it was supremely about Jesus.

The True and Greater Bread God Offers His People

Joseph—like Asa, Abraham, and Job—is another example of God blessing after a trial is endured. Joseph's brothers sold him into slavery when he was seventeen, and they did not see him again until he was thirty-nine.[40] Joseph and his brothers were apart for twenty-two years. For Jesus and His brethren, the Jews, it has been over two thousand years.

While Joseph and his brothers were apart, several things took place. Joseph went from being the lowly, rejected brother to the revered ruler.

> Genesis 41:38—"Pharaoh said to his servants, 'Can we find such a one as this, a man in whom is the Spirit of God?'"

The way Pharaoh spoke of Joseph looks forward to, "Jesus, being filled with the Holy Spirit" (Luke 4:1).

> Genesis 41:39–40—"Then Pharaoh said to Joseph...'There is no one as discerning and wise as you. You shall be over my house, and all my people shall be ruled according to your word; only in regard to the throne will I be greater than you.'"

Joseph was over everyone and everything except Pharaoh, like Jesus is over everyone and everything except God the Father. First Corinthians 15:27 says, "'[the Father] has put all things under [Jesus'] feet.' But when [the Father] says 'all things are put under Him,' it is evident that He who put all things under Him is excepted."

Genesis 41:42–43—"Then Pharaoh took his signet ring off his hand and put it on Joseph's hand; and he clothed him in garments of fine linen and put a gold chain around his neck. And he had him ride in the second chariot which he had; and they cried out before him, 'Bow the knee!' So he set him over all the land of Egypt."

Pharaoh exalted Joseph, and every knee was made to bow to him. The Father does the same for His Son: "God has highly exalted Him and given Him the name which is above every name, that at the name of Jesus every knee should bow, of those in heaven, and of those on earth, and of those under the earth" (Philippians 2:9–10).

When Joseph's brothers rejected him, they had no idea what would happen later. When the Jews rejected Jesus, they also had no idea of what was to come. "The last will be first" (Matthew 19:30, 20:16), and "the humble will be exalted" (Matthew 23:12). Joseph is a good example of these verses, but the greatest fulfillment takes place with Christ.

Genesis 41:55—"So when all the land of Egypt was famished, the people cried to Pharaoh for bread. Then Pharaoh said to all the Egyptians, 'Go to Joseph; whatever he says to you, do.'"

The Egyptians began to starve, and Pharaoh directed them to Joseph. Although Joseph could say to the people, "Look to me, and be saved, all you ends of the earth," (Isaiah 45:22), only Jesus can say these words in the true and greater sense. Joseph gave the people physical life, but Jesus offers eternal life.

> Genesis 47:13–19—"*There was no bread* in all the land; for the famine was very severe…Joseph gathered up all the money…in Egypt and Canaan, for the grain. All the Egyptians came to Joseph and said, '*Give us bread*, for *why should we die?*'
> Joseph said, 'Give your livestock, and *I will give you bread* for your livestock if the money is gone.' They brought their livestock to Joseph, and *Joseph gave them bread*…Thus *he fed them with bread.*
> They came to him the next year and said…'There is nothing left in the sight of my lord but our bodies and our lands. *Why should we die* before your eyes? Buy us and our land… *for bread*…that *we may live and not die.*'"

Bread is mentioned seven times, serving as the focus of the verses. Three times the people asked for bread so they would not die. Regardless of the amount of bread they ate, they still died some years later. In light of eternity, were their lives really lengthened? No. God is not primarily concerned with temporarily extending people's lives. He does not offer bread that adds a few more decades of life. There is a true and greater Bread God gives His people.

Jesus said, "*I am the bread of life*. He who comes to Me *shall never hunger*...If anyone eats of this bread, *he will live forever*; and the bread that I shall give is My flesh, which *I shall give for the life of the world*." (John 6:35, 51). The years Joseph added to people's lives cannot compare to the eternal life Jesus provides. John 6:27–29 records:

> "*Do not labor* for the food which perishes, but *for the food which endures to everlasting life*, which the Son of Man will give you, because God the Father has set His seal on Him."
>
> Then they said to Him, "What shall we do, that we may work the works of God?"
>
> Jesus answered and said to them, "This is the work of God, that *you believe in Him whom He sent*."

Joseph gave the Egyptians bread in exchange for money, livestock, and even their bodies. They sacrificed everything (they did "labor") for bread that perished. Jesus freely offers eternal life. He said the "work of God" is believing in Him.

The account with Joseph reveals one of the most important lessons to remember during trials. God is not primarily concerned with adding more years to our lives. Instead, He wants to give people the Bread of Life. If you do not understand this, then a trial that threatens your life or the life of a loved one, cannot help but produce depression, bitterness, or unbelief. Although if you understand God desires to give you eternal life, then even the end of your earthly life can be faced with joy and thankfulness.

The Greatest Act of Evil
God Meant for Good

Genesis 41:56 says, "The famine was over all the face of the earth." Joseph was the savior of the known world in his day. He did not understand what God was doing during his trials, but he looked back later and understood the end intended by the Lord. When he reconciled with his brothers he told them:

> Genesis 50:20—"But as for you, *you meant evil against me; but God meant it for good*, in order to bring it about as it is this day, *to save many people alive.*"

Joseph spoke the truth, but only Jesus can say these words in the true and greatest sense: "The world meant evil against Me, but God meant it for good, in order to save many people eternally." The worst act of evil did not take place against Joseph. It took place against Jesus. The greatest act God meant for good did not take place through Joseph. It took place through Jesus. Joseph accomplished much good, but how much greater was the good Jesus accomplished? God had an intended end in Joseph's suffering, but think of the greater end God intended through Jesus' suffering. Joseph saved many people physically, but how many more people has Jesus saved in the only way that truly matters—spiritually? What Joseph did—as great as it was—pales in comparison to what Jesus did.

Whether Joseph understood it, everything that happened to him was only secondarily about him. Supremely, it was about Jesus. In the same way, whether we understand it, everything that happens to us is only secondarily about us. Supremely, it is about Jesus. Perhaps we will be able to look back as Joseph did and see the good God brought from our trials—if not on this side of heaven, then in the next life.

Conclusion

Hebrews 11:1 says, "Faith is the substance of things hoped for, the evidence of things not seen." This verse was true in Abraham, Job, and Joseph's lives in a way we will never understand. Moses wrote the first five books of the Bible, but these men lived before he was born. They faced trials without Scripture at their disposal. They could not be encouraged by the heroes of the faith. Abraham and Joseph were busy being two of those heroes (Hebrews 11:8–11, 17–19, 22).

We, on the other hand, have the entirety of God's Word available to us. Even if we do not understand what God is doing, we can walk by faith as we lean on these truths:

- A spiritual, eternal perspective allows trials to be viewed with joy (James 1:2, 1 Peter 1:6).

- Trials test our faith and prove the genuineness of it (1 Peter 1:7).
- Trials produce patience which produces maturity (James 1:3–4).
- There is blessing for enduring trials, whether in this life or the next (James 1:12, 5:11).
- There is an end intended by the Lord—He works all things together for good (James 5:11, Romans 8:28).
- During trials God is still being very compassionate and merciful (James 5:11).
- Jesus, the bread from heaven, gives us eternal life (John 6:32, 47).

Our suffering is not meaningless. God loves us. He is for us. He works in our best interests. When we become discouraged during trials, these are the truths we need to remember.

Questions

1. How do the lives of Abraham and Joseph exalt Christ?

2. What other examples in Scripture can you think of individuals suffering which brought forth good?

3. In what ways is Jesus the Bread of Life? Why did He use this title for Himself?

4. Which of the bulleted truths at the end of the chapter most encourage you? Why?

5. After coming to the end of *Enduring Trials God's Way*, what other truths would you add to the bulleted list?

6. How do you view trials differently now than you did prior to reading this book?

7. Second Corinthians 4:17 says, "For our light affliction, which is but for a moment, is working for us a far more exceeding and eternal weight of glory." Break down this verse and lay out your trial:

   A. "For our light affliction"—Describe your trial.

   B. "Which is but for a moment"—Draw a timeline of eternity, with your life indicated on it. Then identify the length of the trial. Consider the relationship of the trial to the length of your life and the length of eternity.

C. "Is working for us a far more exceeding"—What is this trial accomplishing in your life on this side of heaven?

D. "And eternal weight of glory"—How is this trial preparing you for eternity? Provide three verses discussing the rewards available in the next life.

I.

II.

III.

About the Author

S cott is the senior pastor of Woodland Christian Church in Woodland, Washington and a conference speaker. He and his wife, Katie, grew up together in northern California, and God has blessed them with seven children.

You can contact Pastor Scott or learn more about him at the following:

- Email: scott@scottlapierre.org
- Website: www.scottlapierre.org
- Facebook: @ScottLaPierreAuthor
- YouTube: @ScottLaPierre
- Twitter: @PastorWCC
- Instagram: @PastorWCC

Subscribe to Pastor Scott's Newsletter

Receive free chapters of Pastor Scott's books, videos of his conference messages, and updates about his ministry by subscribing to his newsletter:

https://www.scottlapierre.org/subscribe/

Would You Like to Invite Pastor Scott to Speak at Your Event?

You can expect:

- •Professionally prepared and delivered messages
- Handouts with lessons and discussion questions
- Copies of Pastor Scott's books to offer as gifts to increase registrations (if you desire)
- Prompt replies to communication
- Advertising of your event on Pastor Scott's social media

Schedule for Conferences—Typically there are one or two sessions on Friday evening, and three or four sessions on Saturday, but there is flexibility: conferences can be spread over three days or kept to one day, and Q&A sessions can be added.

Outreach—Consider viewing the conference as an outreach to share Christ with your community. Pastor Scott can run a Facebook ad, and/or set up a Facebook event page for those in the church to share with others.

For more information, including sample messages and endorsements, please visit:

www.scottlapierre.org/conferences-and-speaking.

Marriage God's Way:
A Biblical Recipe for Healthy,
Joyful, Christ-Centered Relationships

Nearly everything in life comes with instructions, from the cell phones we use to the automobiles we drive. Yet when it comes to marriage, many people struggle without proper guidance. Pastor Scott presents the needed biblical instructions combined with:

- Personal stories and application to daily life
- Explanations of the roles and responsibilities God has given husbands and wives
- Answers to common questions about godly love and how to show it, headship and submission, intimacy, and establishing an indestructible foundation for your relationship

Endorsed by well-known ministry leaders:

- **Tedd Tripp:** "The reader will be richly rewarded."
  —Best-selling author of *Shepherding a Child's Heart*
- **Scott Brown:** "This is what every marriage needs!"
  —Founder of The National Center for Family-Integrated Churches and author of *A Theology of the Family*

A Father Offers His Son:
The True and Greater Sacrifice Revealed Through Abraham and Isaac

Have you ever wondered why God asked Abraham to sacrifice his son in Genesis 22? The Angel stopped Abraham showing God did not intend for him to kill Isaac, but what did God desire? God wanted to test Abraham,  and readers will discover the account primarily reveals:

- In human terms what God would do with His Son two thousand years later
- The many ways Abraham and Isaac are a picture of God and His Son
- The tremendous love of God shown through Christ's sacrifice

Endorsed by ministry leaders:

- **Dr. Paul Benware:** "I highly recommend this work that will deepen your appreciation for what the Father and Son went through."
  —Professor, Pastor, Speaker, and Author
- **Cary Green:** "As a jeweler holds a gemstone and examines each priceless, shining facet, Pastor Scott holds high this picture of heaven's sacrificial love and examines every detail."
  —Senior Pastor, Missionary, and Church Planter

Notes

1 "G3579 - xenizō – Strong's Greek Lexicon (KJV)." Blue Letter Bible. Accessed 30 Jun, 2017. https://www.blueletterbible.org//lang/lexicon/lexicon.cfm?Strongs=G3579&t=KJV

2 "G4045 - peripiptō – Strong's Greek Lexicon (KJV)." Blue Letter Bible. Accessed 1 Nov, 2017. https://www.blueletterbible.org//lang/lexicon/lexicon.cfm?Strongs=G4045&t=KJV

3 Park, David. "NATO Video Captures Czech Pilot's Bird Strike." News Expats. https://news.expats.cz/weekly-czech-news/nato-video-captures-czech-pilot-birdstrike/ Nov. 25, 2015.

4 "G2233 - hēgeomai – Strong's Greek Lexicon (KJV)." Blue Letter Bible. Accessed 1 Nov, 2017. https://www.blueletterbible.org//lang/lexicon/lexicon.cfm?Strongs=G2233&t=KJV

5 Bridges, Jerry, *Trusting God*. NavPress, Reprint Edition 2017, p. 149.

6 "G5281 - hypomonē – Strong's Greek Lexicon (KJV)." Blue Letter Bible. Accessed 1 Jul, 2017. https://www.blueletterbible.org//lang/lexicon/lexicon.cfm?Strongs=G5281&t=KJV

7 "G5046 - teleios – Strong's Greek Lexicon (KJV)." Blue Letter Bible. Accessed 1 Jul, 2017. https://www.blueletterbible.org//lang/lexicon/lexicon.cfm?Strongs=G5046&t=KJV

8 "G3648 - holoklēros – Strong's Greek Lexicon (KJV)." Blue Letter Bible. Accessed 4 Jul, 2017. https://www.blueletterbible.org//lang/lexicon/lexicon.cfm?Strongs=G3648&t=KJV

9 "G3007 - leipō – Strong's Greek Lexicon (KJV)." Blue Letter Bible. Accessed 4 Jul, 2017. https://www.blueletterbible.org//lang/lexicon/lexicon.cfm?Strongs=G3007&t=KJV

10 "G1722 - en – Strong's Greek Lexicon (KJV)." Blue Letter Bible. Accessed 4 Jul, 2017. https://www.blueletterbible.org//lang/lexicon/lexicon.cfm?Strongs=g1722&t=KJV

[11] "G3367 - mēdeis – Strong's Greek Lexicon (KJV)." Blue Letter Bible. Accessed 4 Jul, 2017. https://www.blueletterbible.org//lang/lexicon/lexicon.cfm?Strongs=G3367&t=KJV

[12] Barclay, William. *"Bible Commentaries – William Barclay's Daily Study Bible James 1."* Study Light. https://www.studylight.org/commentaries/dsb/james-1.html

[13] Shoda, Yuichi; Mischel, Walter; Peake, Philip K. (1990). *"Predicting Adolescent Cognitive and Self-Regulatory Competencies from Preschool Delay of Gratification: Identifying Diagnostic Conditions."* Developmental Psychology. 26 (6): 978–986. doi:10.1037/0012-1649.26.6.978. Archived from the original (PDF) on October 4, 2011.

[14] Kelly, Douglas. Partakers of Holiness, Tabletalk. October 2004, p. 38.

[15] MacArthur, John. *Matthew 1-7 (The MacArthur New Testament Commentary).* Moody Publishers; New edition. August 8, 1985, p. 88.

[16] "G2192 - echō – Strong's Greek Lexicon (KJV)." Blue Letter Bible. Accessed 4 Jul, 2017. https://www.blueletterbible.org//lang/lexicon/lexicon.cfm?Strongs=G2192&t=KJV

[17] Broger, James. *Self-Confrontation Manual*, Lesson 8, p. 3, Used by Permission of the Biblical Counseling Foundation.

[18] Chapman, Wilbur J. *Revival Sermons* (New York: Fleming H. Revell, 1911), p. 231.

[19] "H7843 – shachath – Strong's Hebrew Lexicon (KJV)." Blue Letter Bible. Accessed Oct 7, 2017. https://www.blueletterbible.org/lang/Lexicon/Lexicon.cfm?strongs=H7843&t=KJV

[20] "H3335 – yatsar – Strong's Hebrew Lexicon (KJV)." Blue Letter Bible. Accessed Oct 7, 2017. https://www.blueletterbible.org/lang/Lexicon/Lexicon.cfm?strongs=H3335&t=KJV

[21] "G1987 - epistamai – Strong's Greek Lexicon (KJV)." Blue Letter Bible. Accessed 30 Jun, 2017. https://www.blueletterbible.org//lang/lexicon/lexicon.cfm?Strongs=G1987&t=KJV

22 "G1097 - ginōskō – Strong's Greek Lexicon (KJV)." Blue Letter Bible. Accessed 30 Jun, 2017. https://www.blueletterbible.org//lang/lexicon/lexicon.cfm?Strongs=G1097&t=KJV

23 "G3986 - peirasmos – Strong's Greek Lexicon (KJV)." Blue Letter Bible. Accessed 30 Jun, 2017. https://www.blueletterbible.org//lang/lexicon/lexicon.cfm?Strongs=G3986&t=KJV

24 "G1383 - dokimion – Strong's Greek Lexicon (KJV)." Blue Letter Bible. Accessed 30 Jun, 2017. https://www.blueletterbible.org//lang/lexicon/lexicon.cfm?Strongs=G1383&t=KJV

25 MacArthur, John F. *The MacArthur Bible Commentary*. Thomas Nelson, c2005, p. 1881.

26 Wells, Tom. *Christian: Take Heart!* Banner of Truth Trust, Carlisle, PA. 1987, p. 150-151.

27 Kempis, Thomas A. http://gracequotes.org/quote/adversities-do-not-make-a-man-frail-they-show-what/

28 Wiersbe, Warren W. *The Wiersbe Bible Commentary: Old Testament*. David C. Cook, 2007, Colorado Springs, p. 86.

29 Muller, George. Back to the Bible, http://www.backtothebible.org/devotions/greatest-gifts-come-through-travail Accessed 01 Jul, 2017.

30 Lenski, R.C.H. *"The Interpretation of the Epistle to the Hebrews and the Epistle of James"* Augsburg Fortress Publishers, October 1, 2008. p. 525.

31 "H5254 - nacah – Strong's Hebrew Lexicon (KJV)." Blue Letter Bible. Accessed 30 Jun, 2017. https://www.blueletterbible.org//lang/lexicon/lexicon.cfm?Strongs=H5254&t=KJV

32 "H3045 - yada` – Strong's Hebrew Lexicon (KJV)." Blue Letter Bible. Accessed 30 Jun, 2017. https://www.blueletterbible.org//lang/lexicon/lexicon.cfm?Strongs=H3045&t=KJV

33 Fawcett, John. *Christ Precious to Those Who Believe*. Bottom of the Hill Publishing, 2013, p165.

[34]Zuck, Roy. "What is the Law of First Mention?" Got Questions. https://www.gotquestions.org/law-of-first-mention.html

[35]The NKJV says "temptation," but most other translations—including the ESV, NASB, and NIV— say, "trials," and it is the Greek word for trials (peirasmos) in James 1:2 and 1 Peter 1:6.

[36]Wiersbe, Warren. *Be Mature (James): Growing Up in Christ (The BE Series Commentary)*. David C. Cook, June 1, 2008. p.165.

[37]Whyte, Dr. Alexander. Our Missions: Friends' Missionary Magazine, Volume 9, Issue 97 - Volume 10, Issue 120. January 1902.

[38]Library of Congress. American Colony in Jerusalem, 1870 to 2006. Accessed Aug 22, 2017. http://www.loc.gov/exhibits/americancolony/amcolony-family.html

[39]Fetke, Tom. *The Hymnal for Worship and Celebration.* "It is Well with my Soul." World Music, c1986, Hymn 493.

[40]Joseph was seventeen years old when sold into slavery (Genesis 37:2). He was "thirty years old when he stood before Pharaoh" (Genesis 41:46). There were seven years of plenty followed by seven years of famine (Genesis 41:29-30). Joseph brought his father, Jacob, into Egypt when there were two years of famine left (Genesis 45:6, 11). This means Joseph was about thirty-nine when he was reunited with his brothers: 30+7+(7-5).